Natural Landscapes
REVERSE
Coloring Book

This book belongs to:

....

....

....

Inspiration

There are no rules! But you can try some of these ideas.

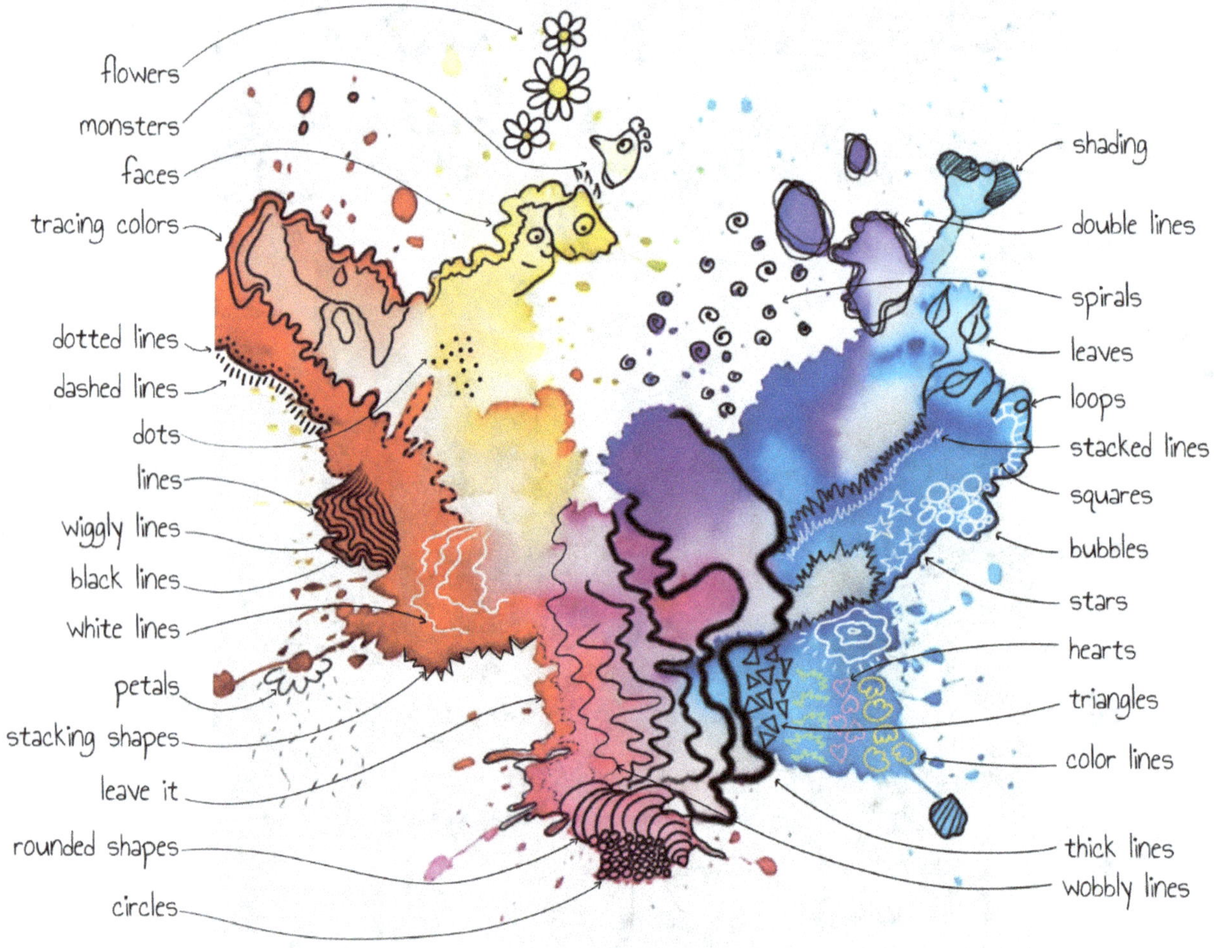

- flowers
- monsters
- faces
- tracing colors
- dotted lines
- dashed lines
- dots
- lines
- wiggly lines
- black lines
- white lines
- petals
- stacking shapes
- leave it
- rounded shapes
- circles
- shading
- double lines
- spirals
- leaves
- loops
- stacked lines
- squares
- bubbles
- stars
- hearts
- triangles
- color lines
- thick lines
- wobbly lines

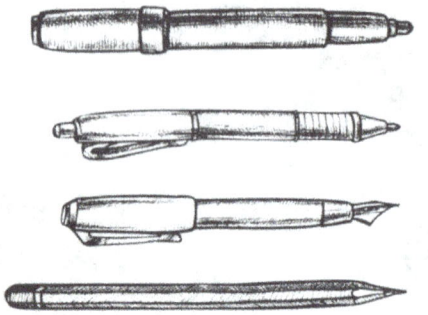

You can use any tool you like. Experiment with different thicknesses, textures and colors. Find out which one you like the most. You'll be suprised by the effect.

Sample drawing

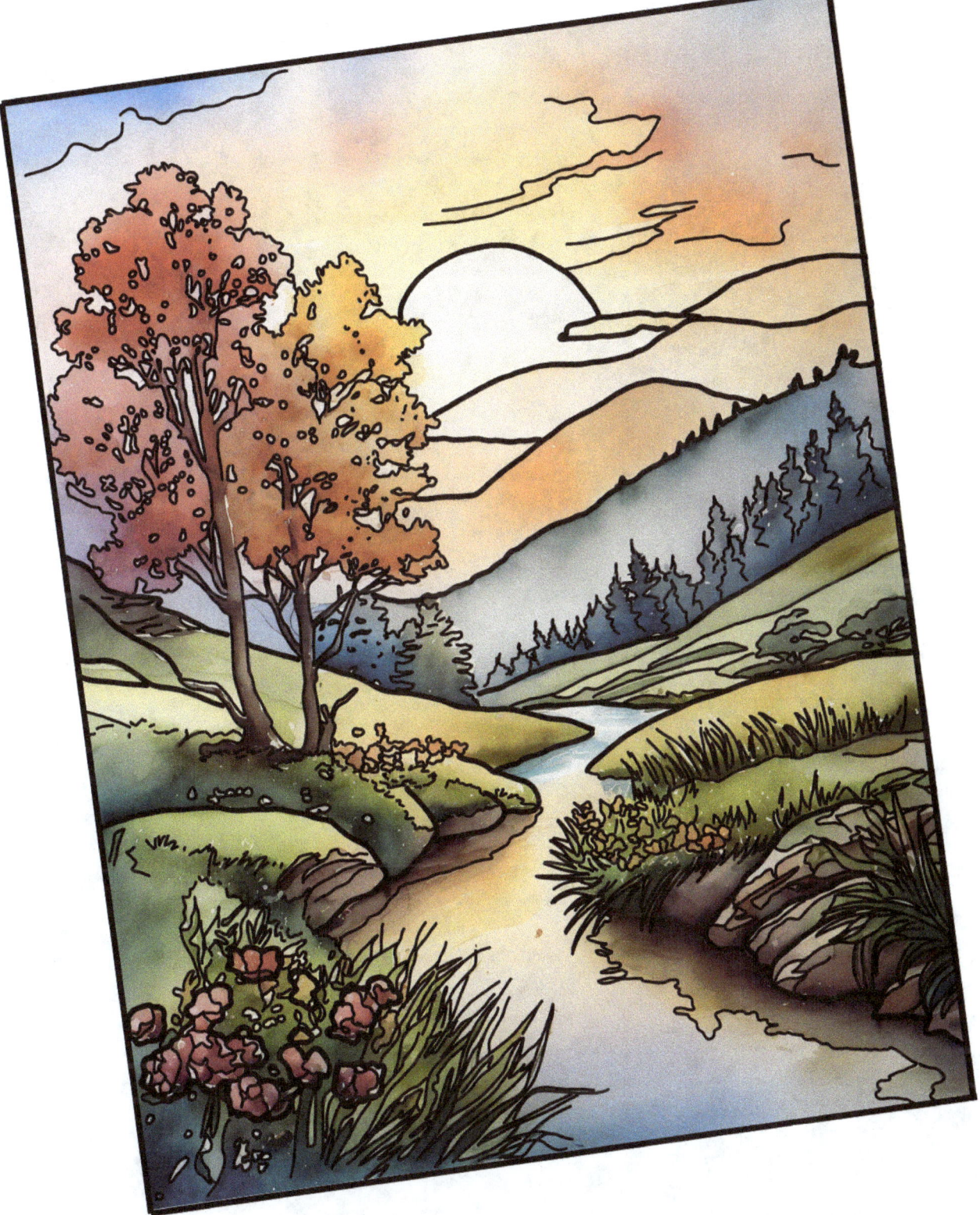

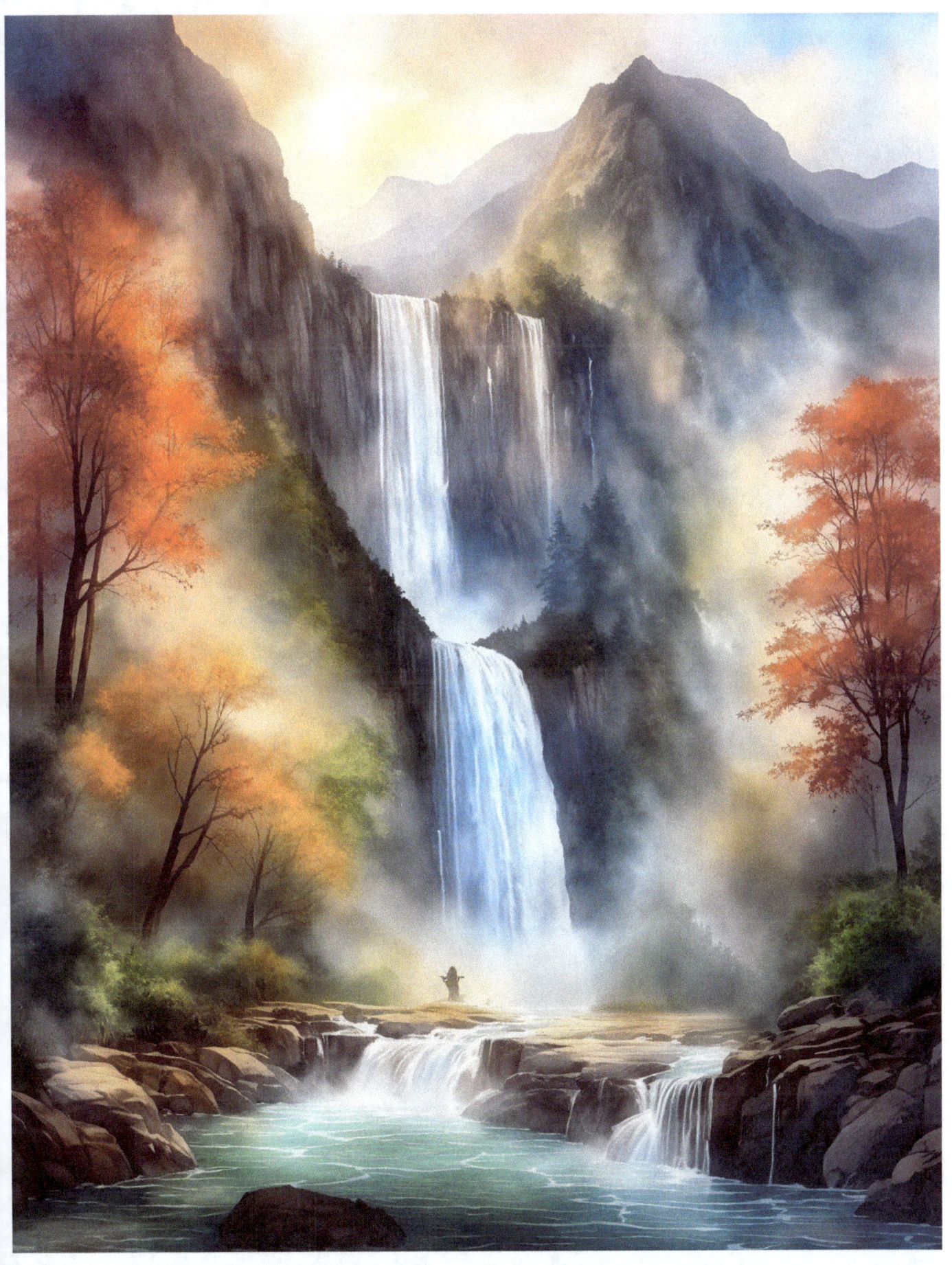

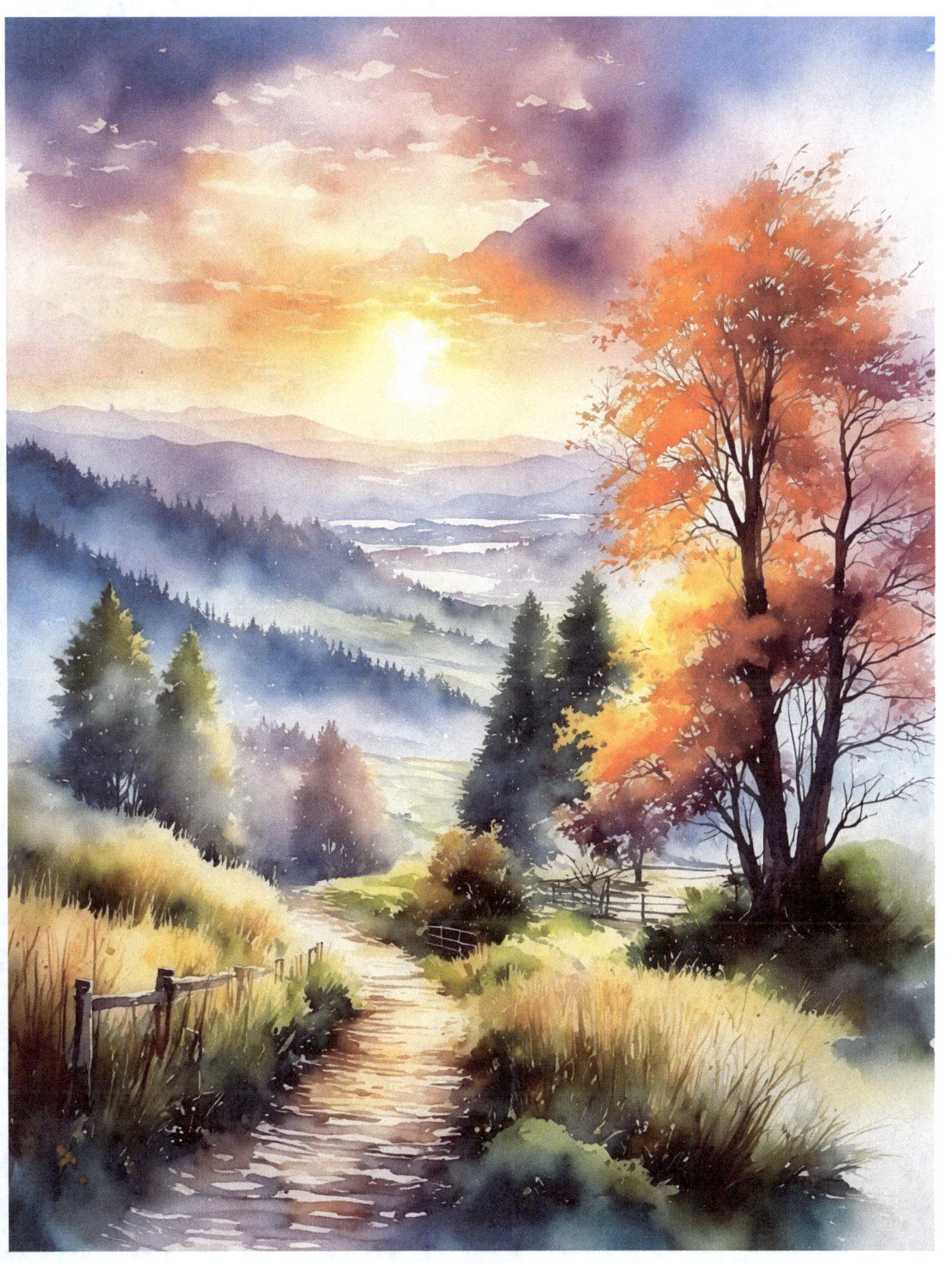

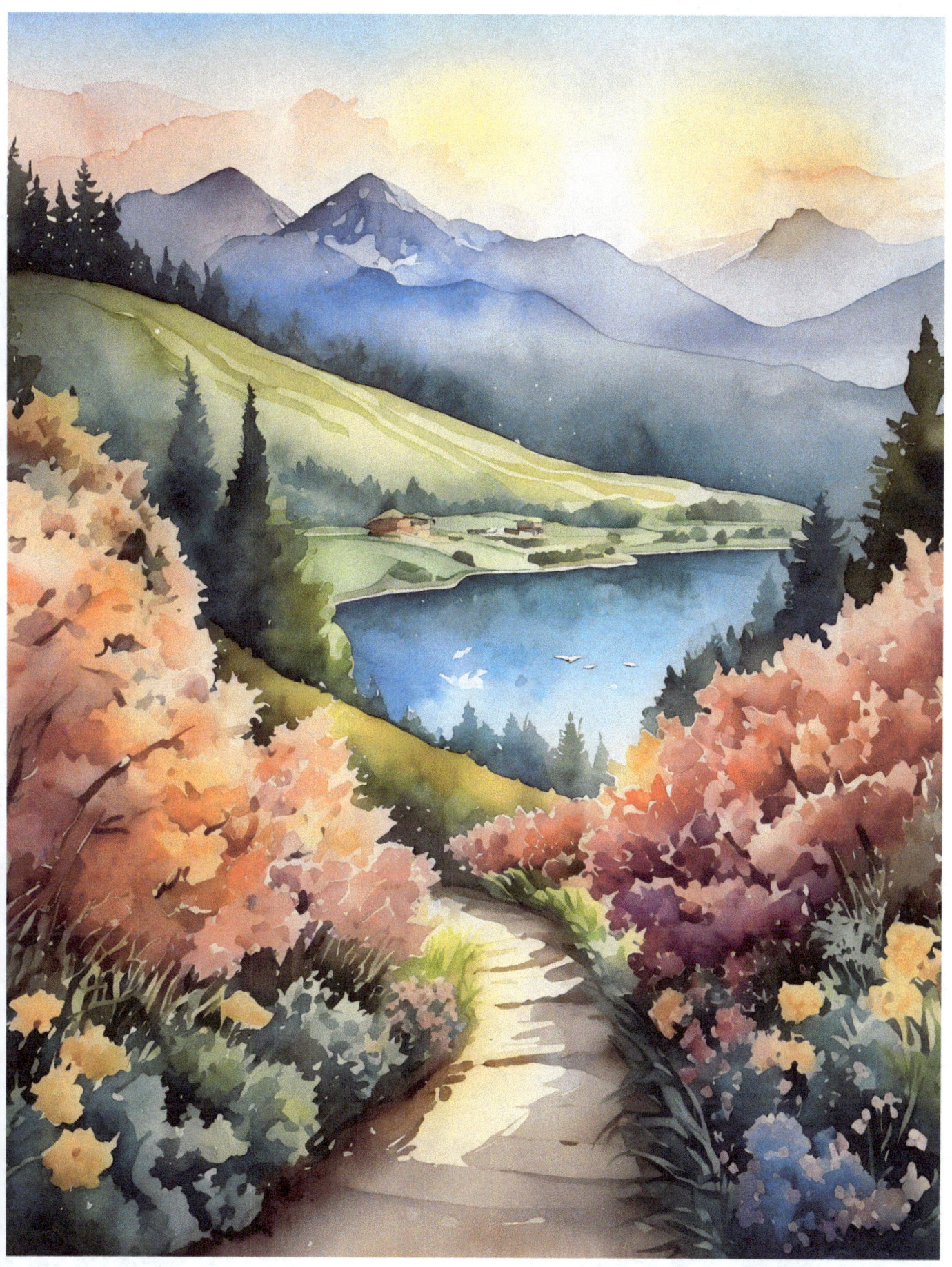

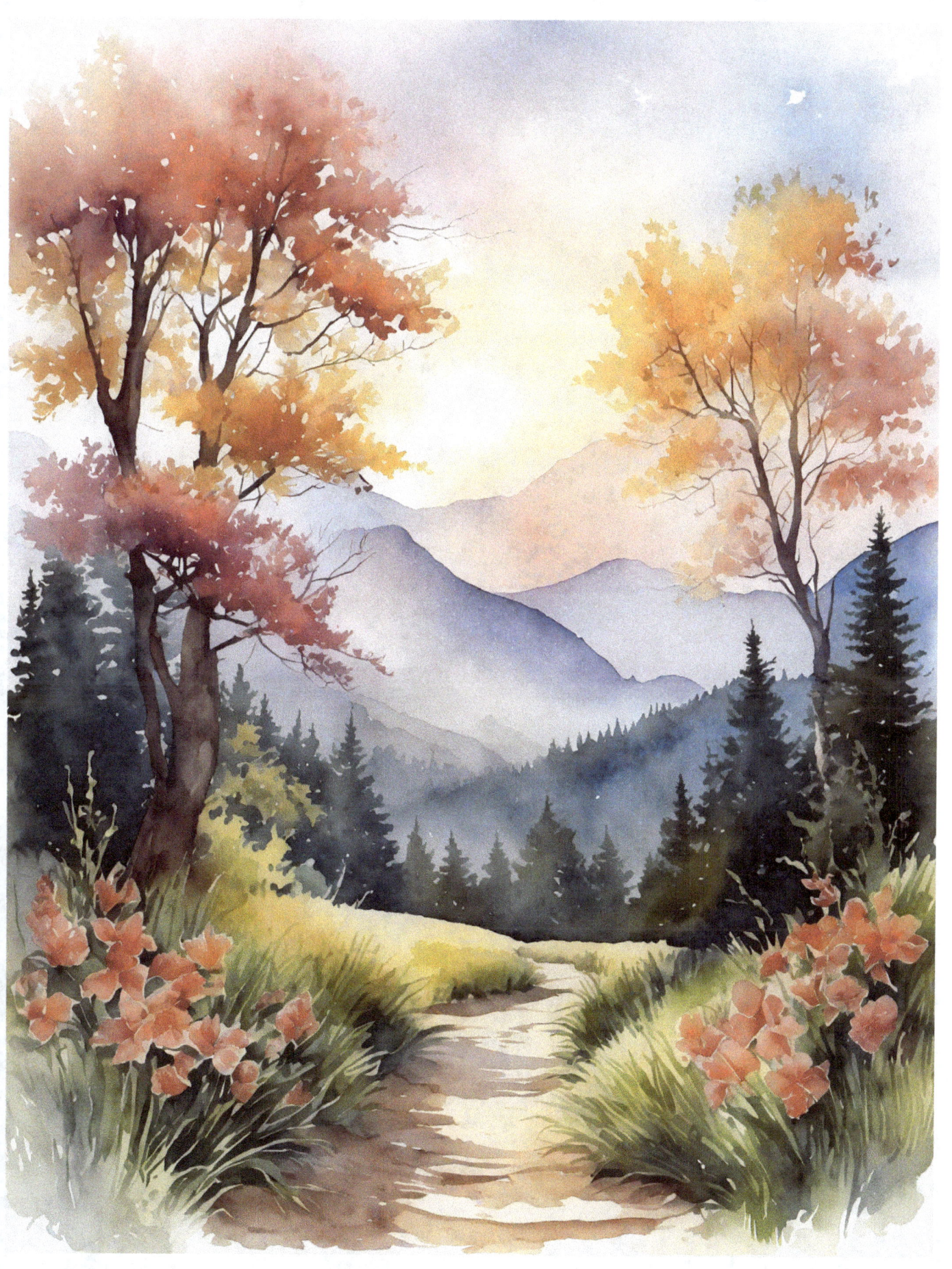

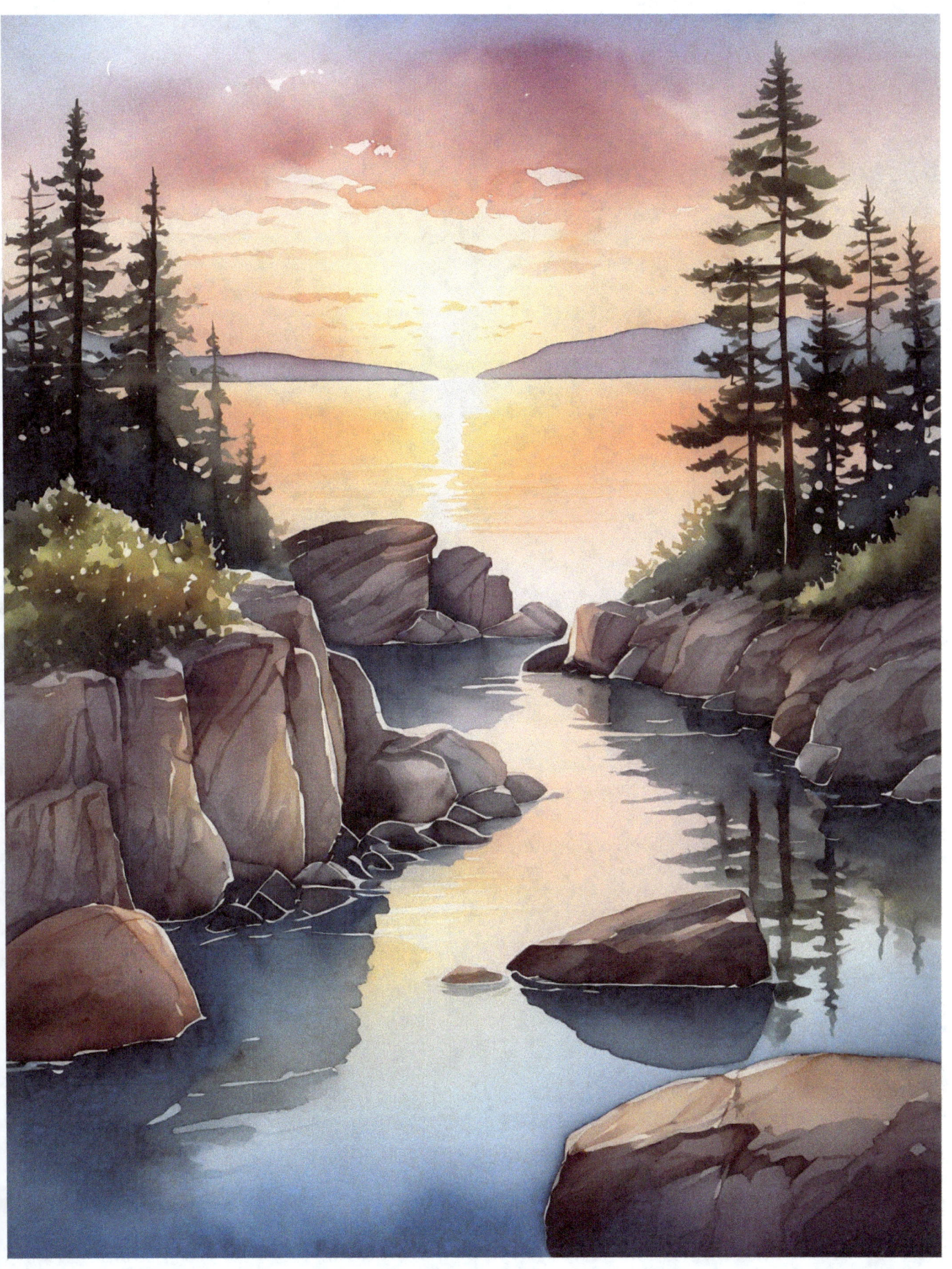

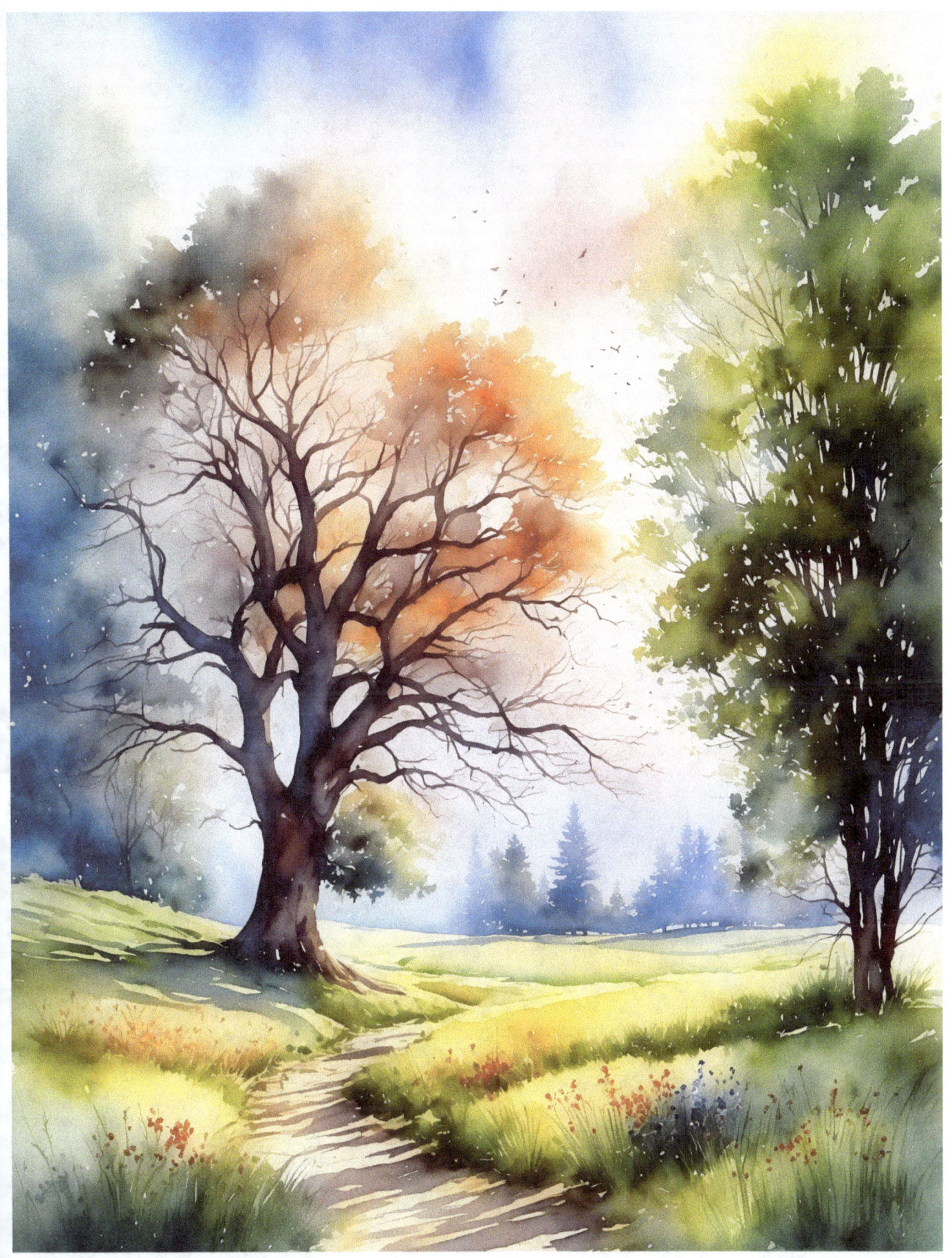

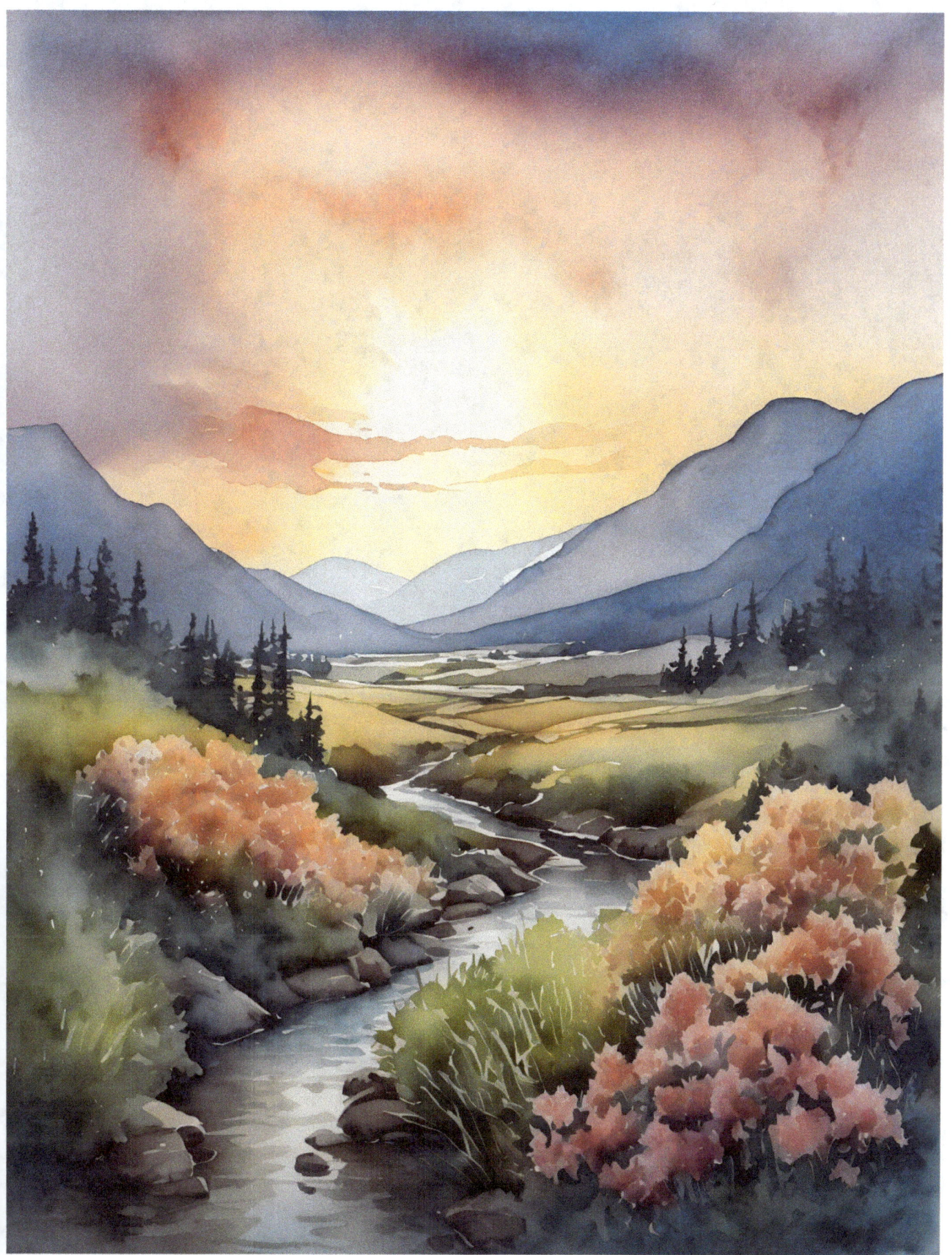

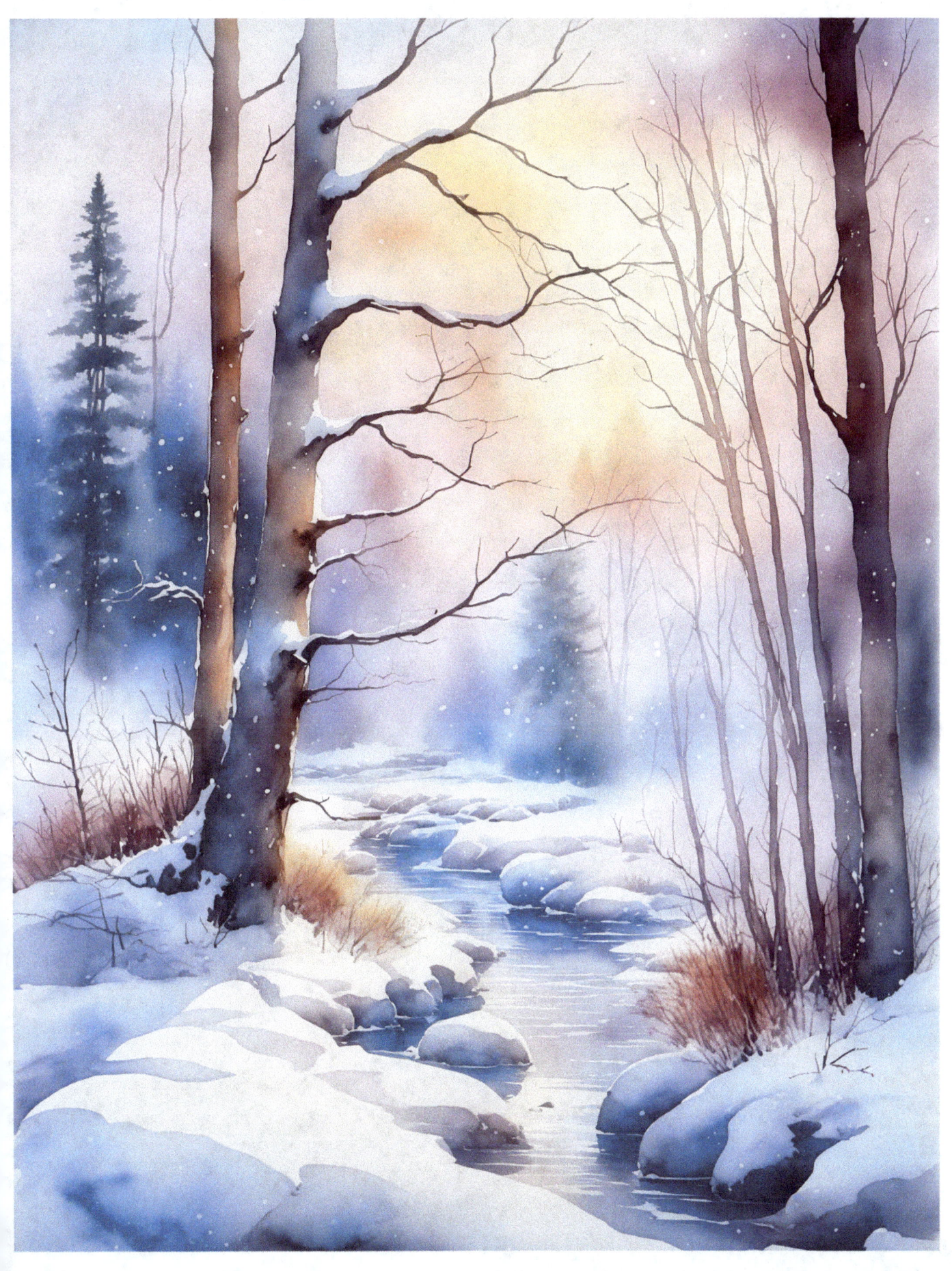

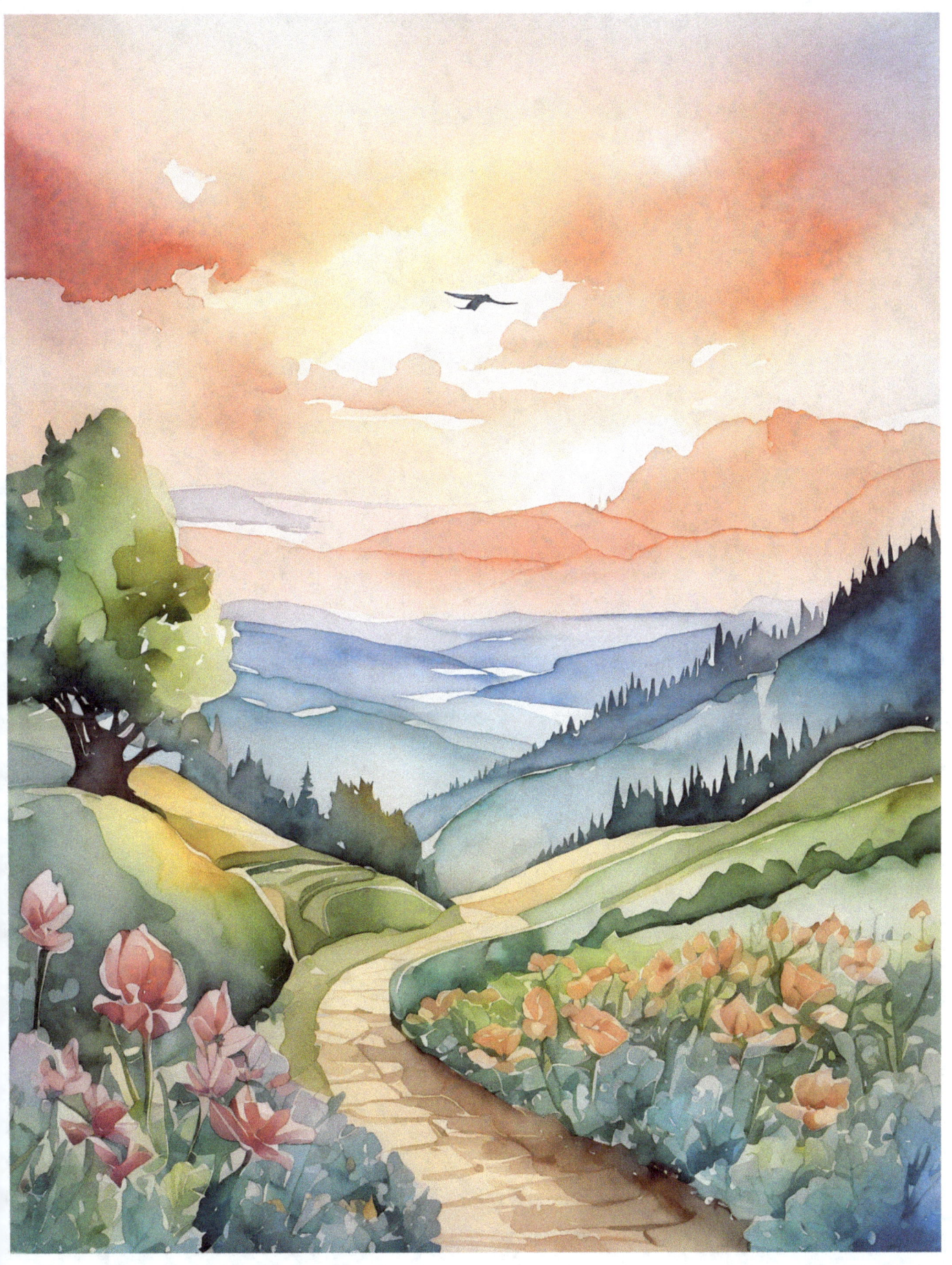

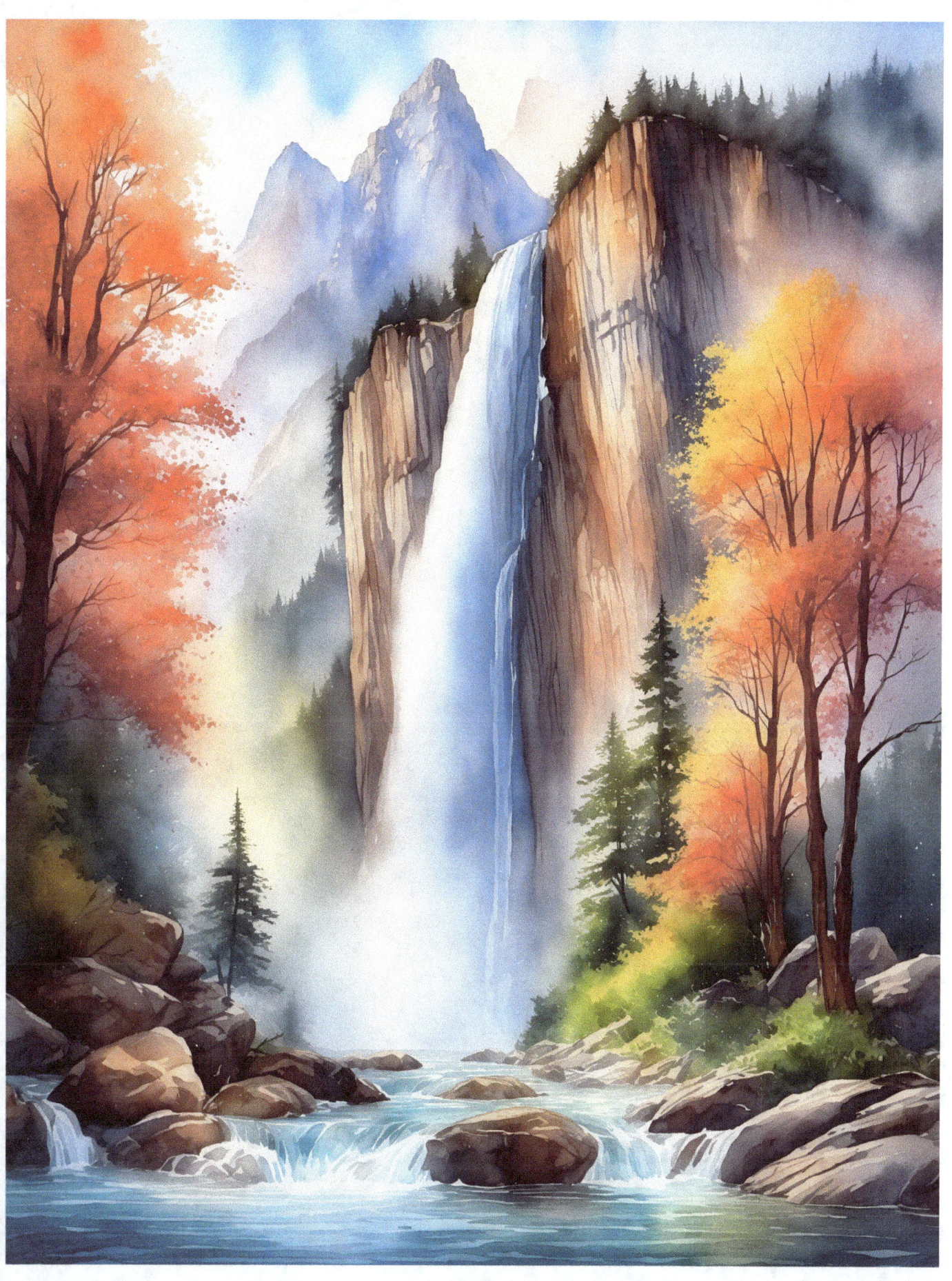

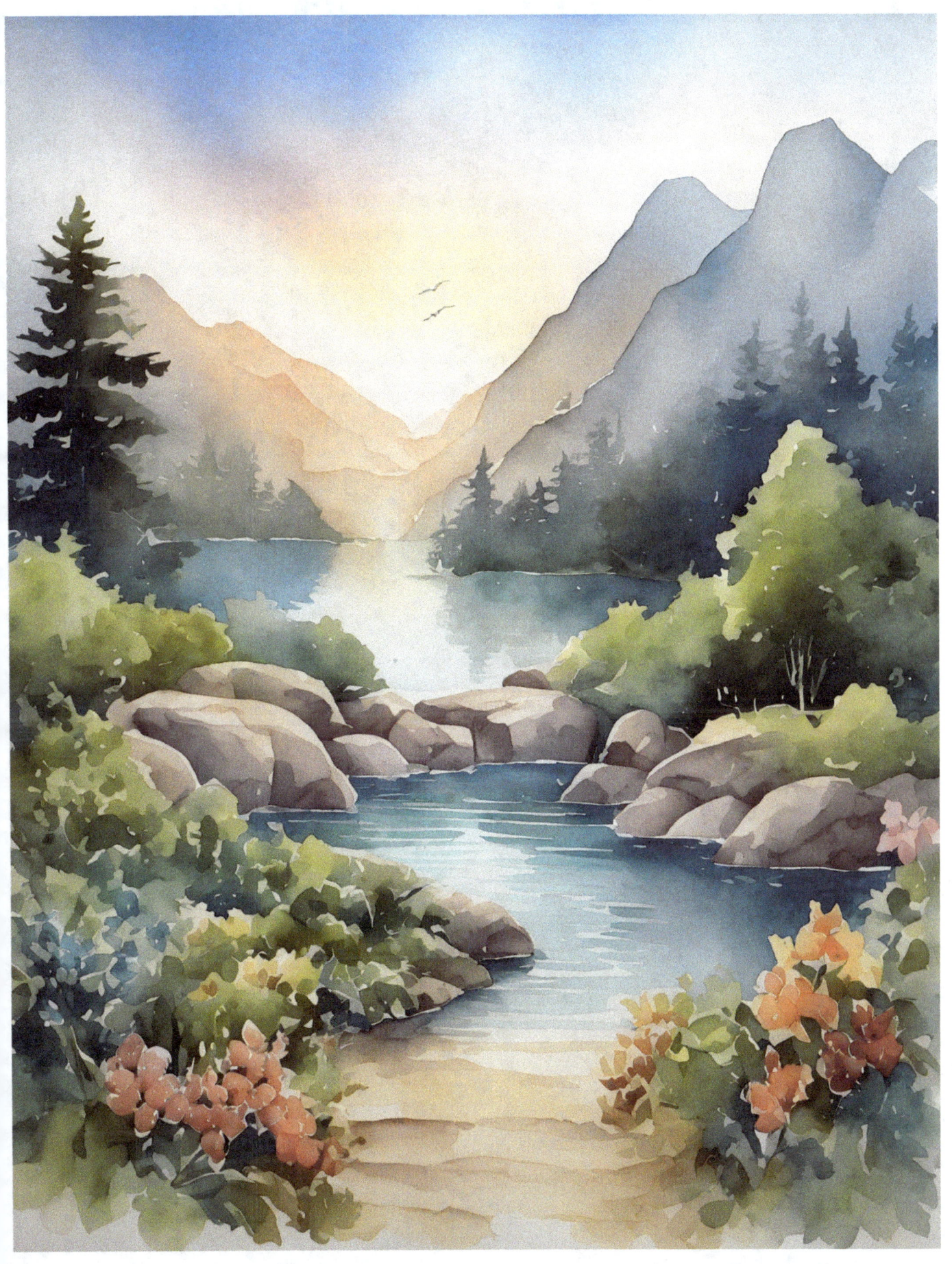

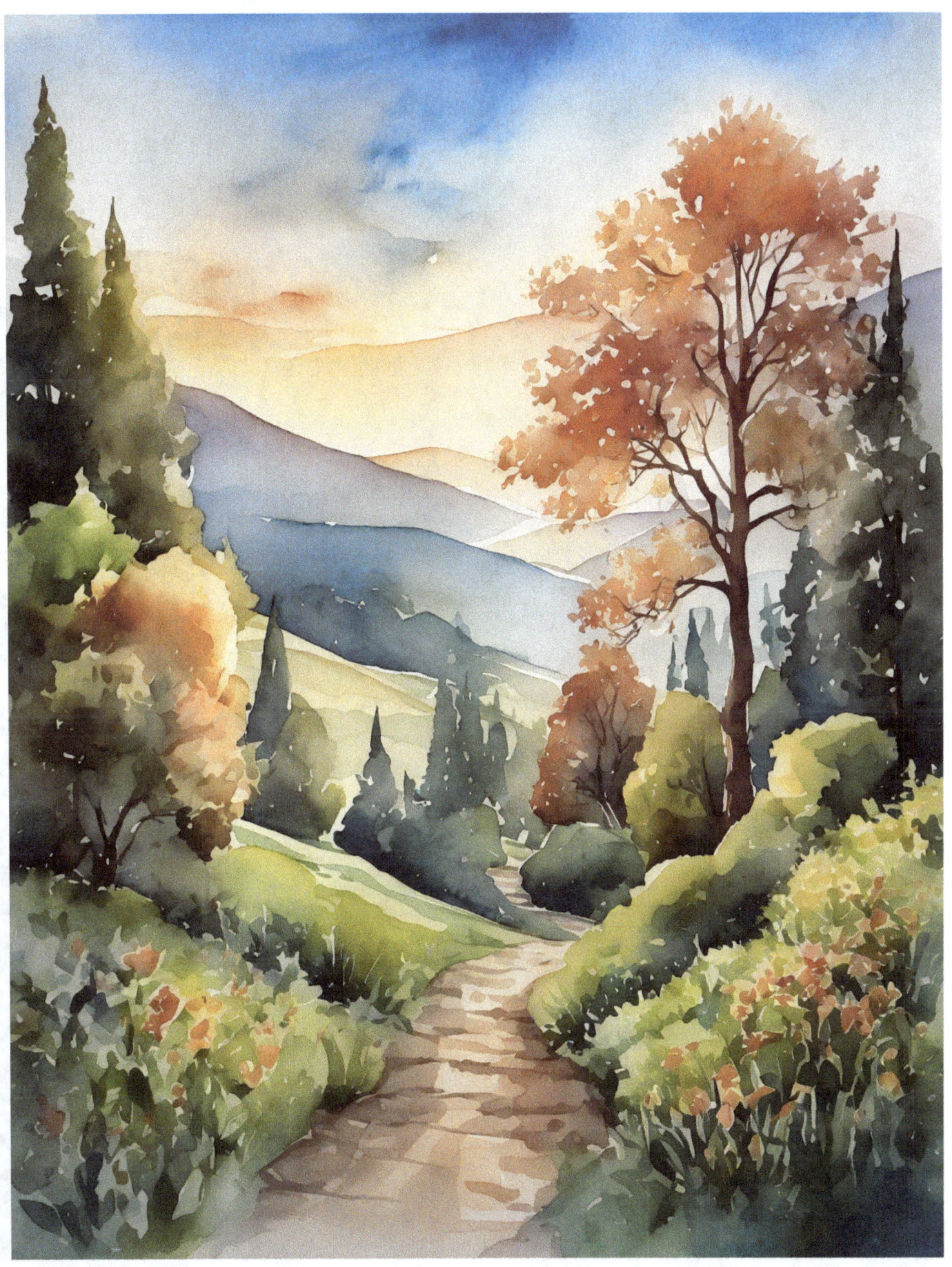

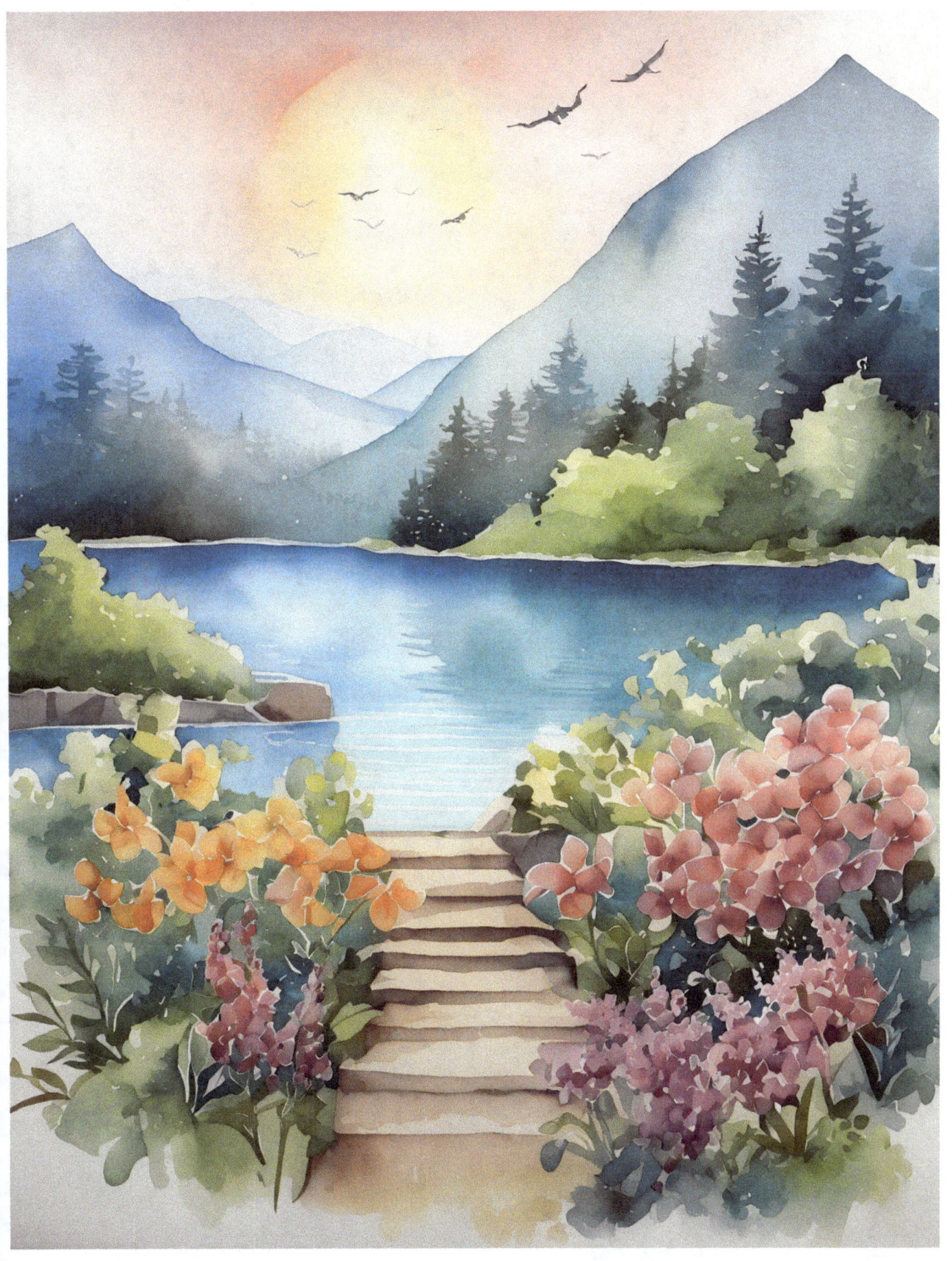

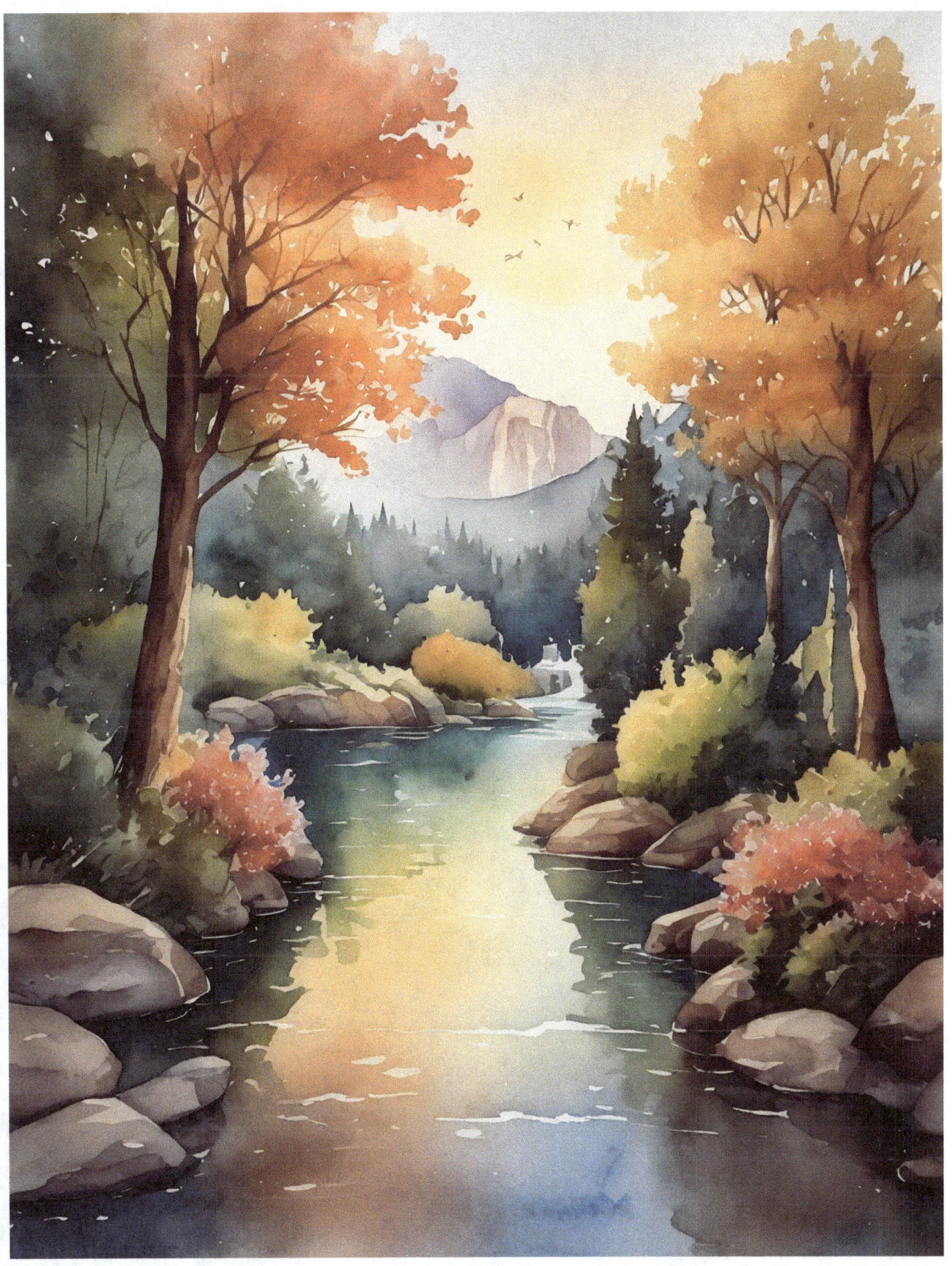

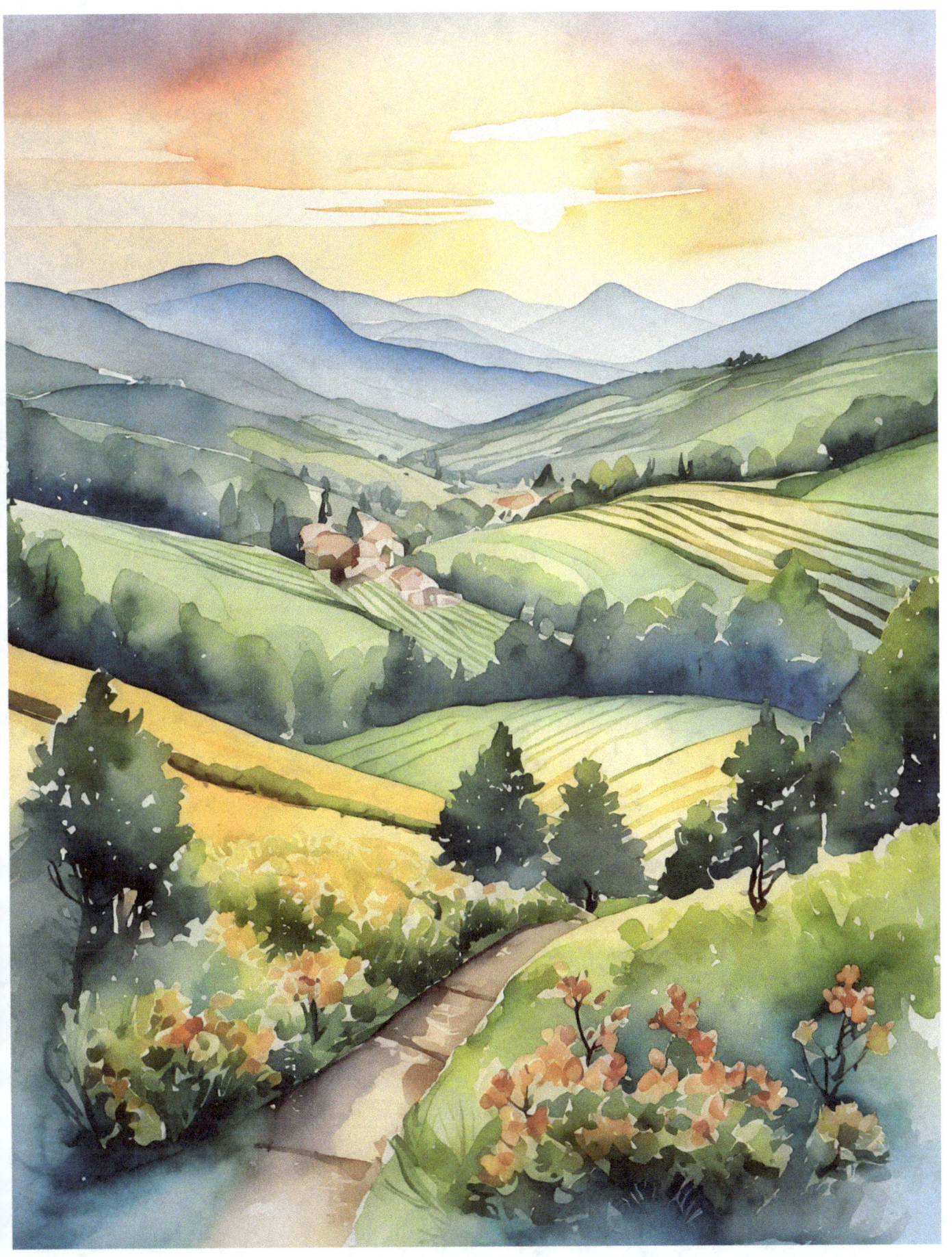

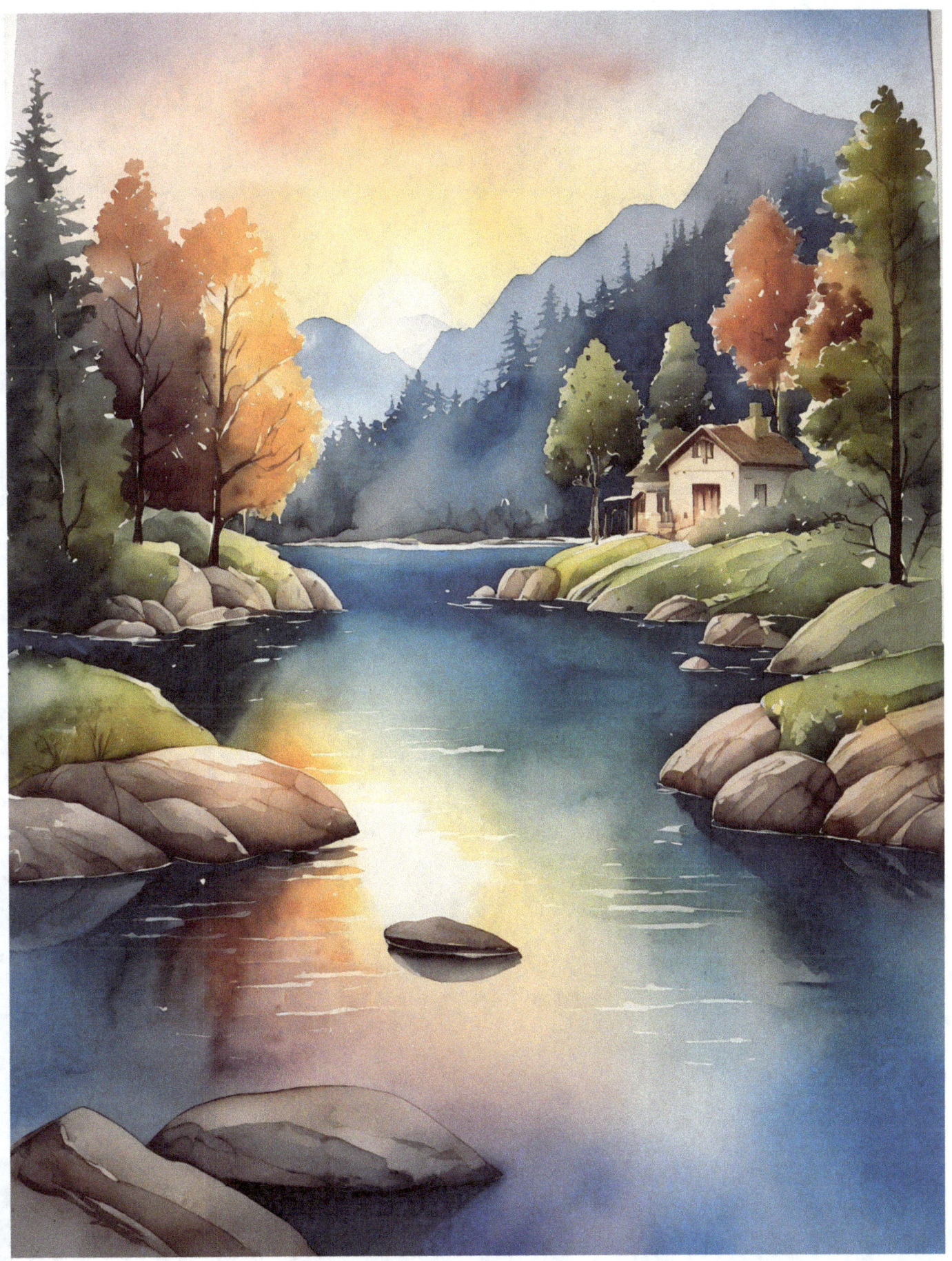

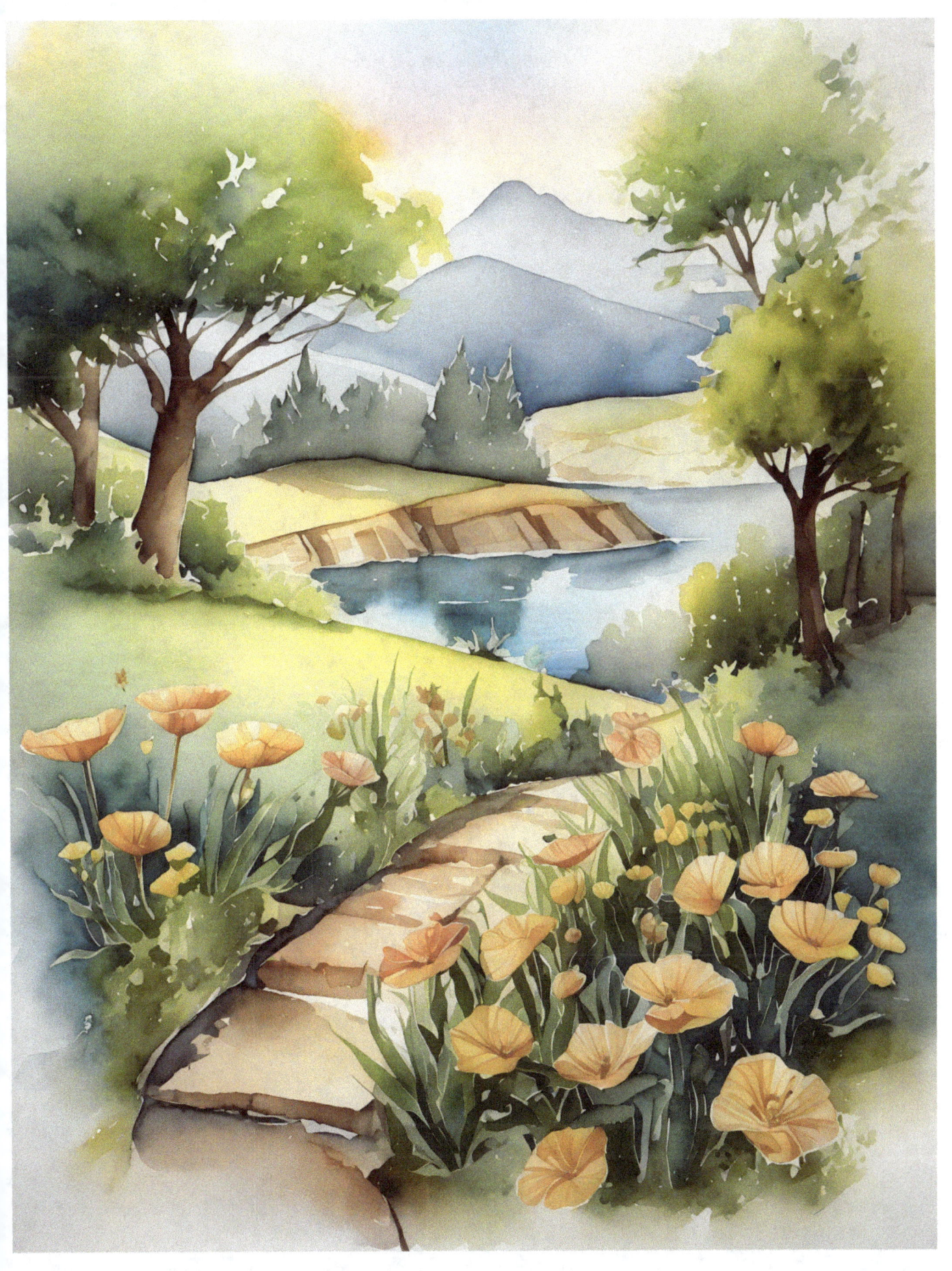

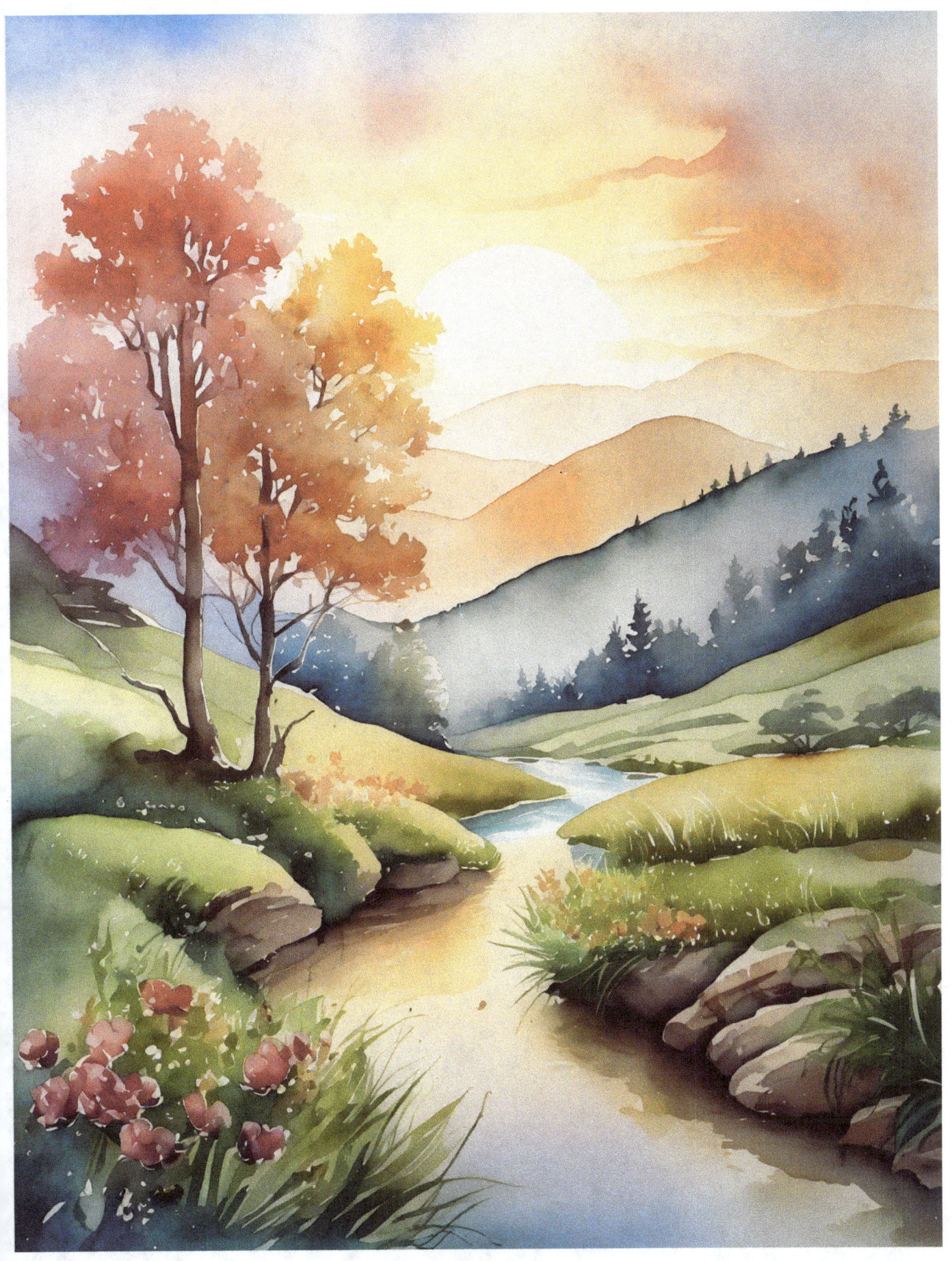

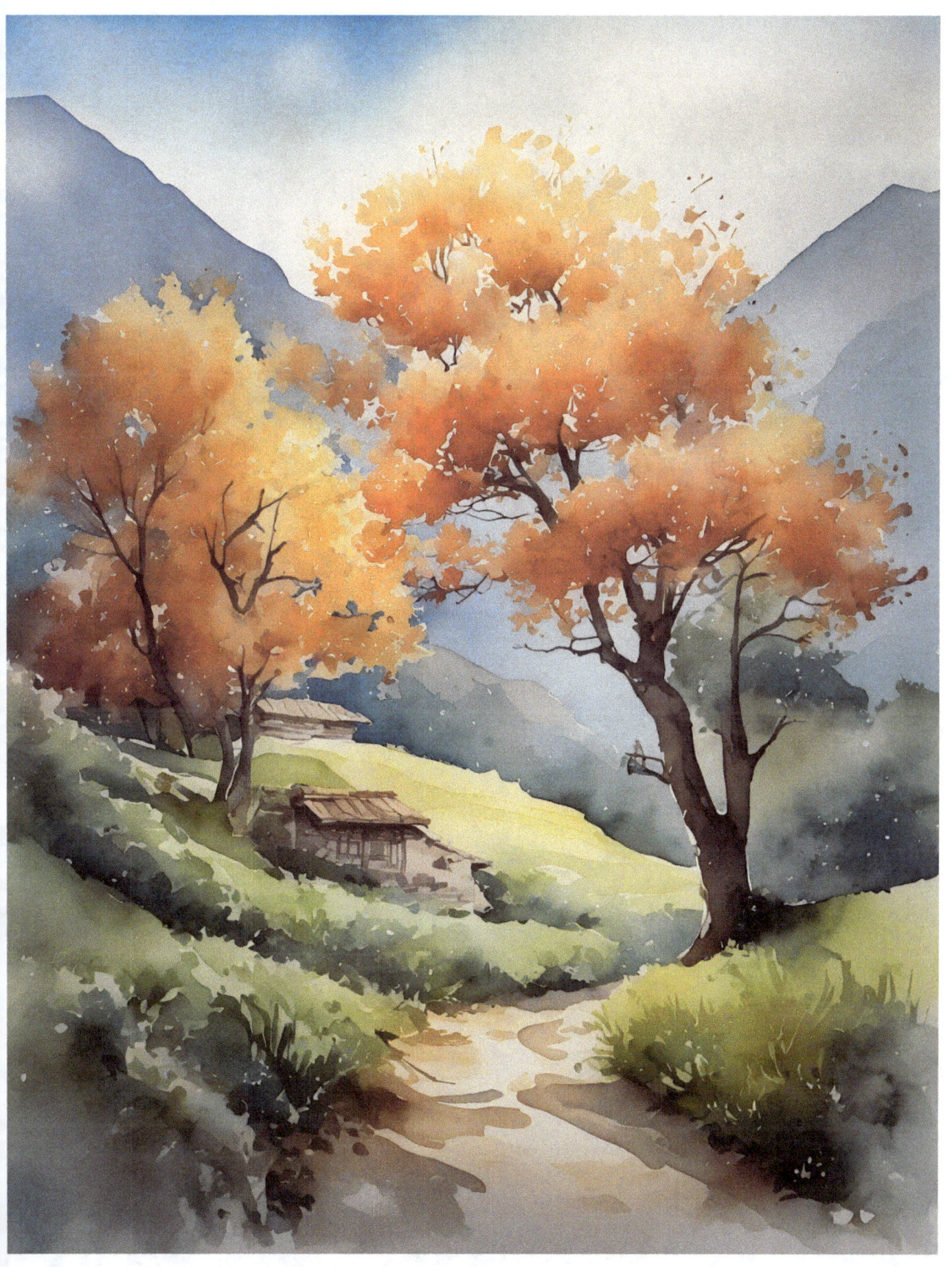

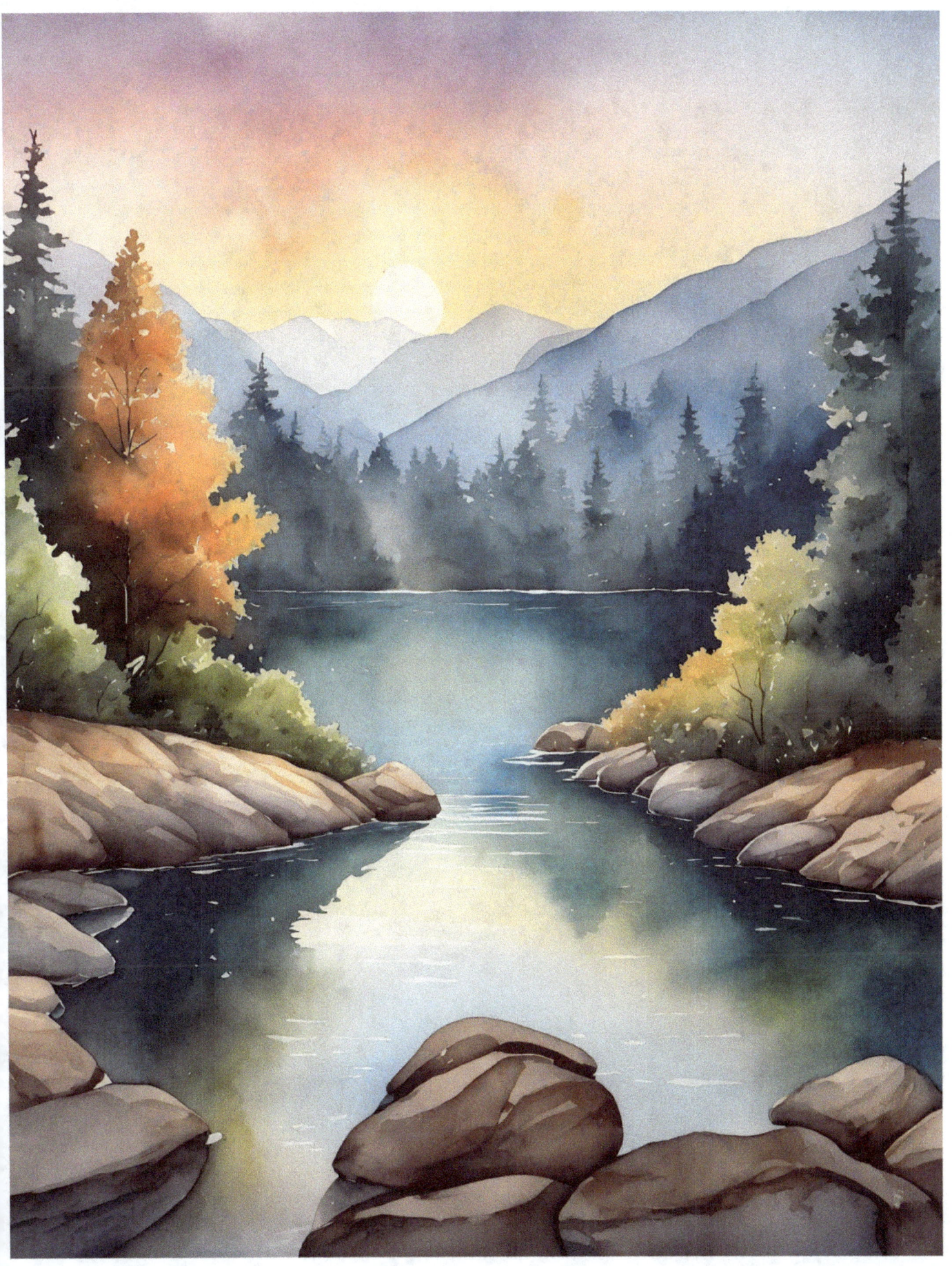

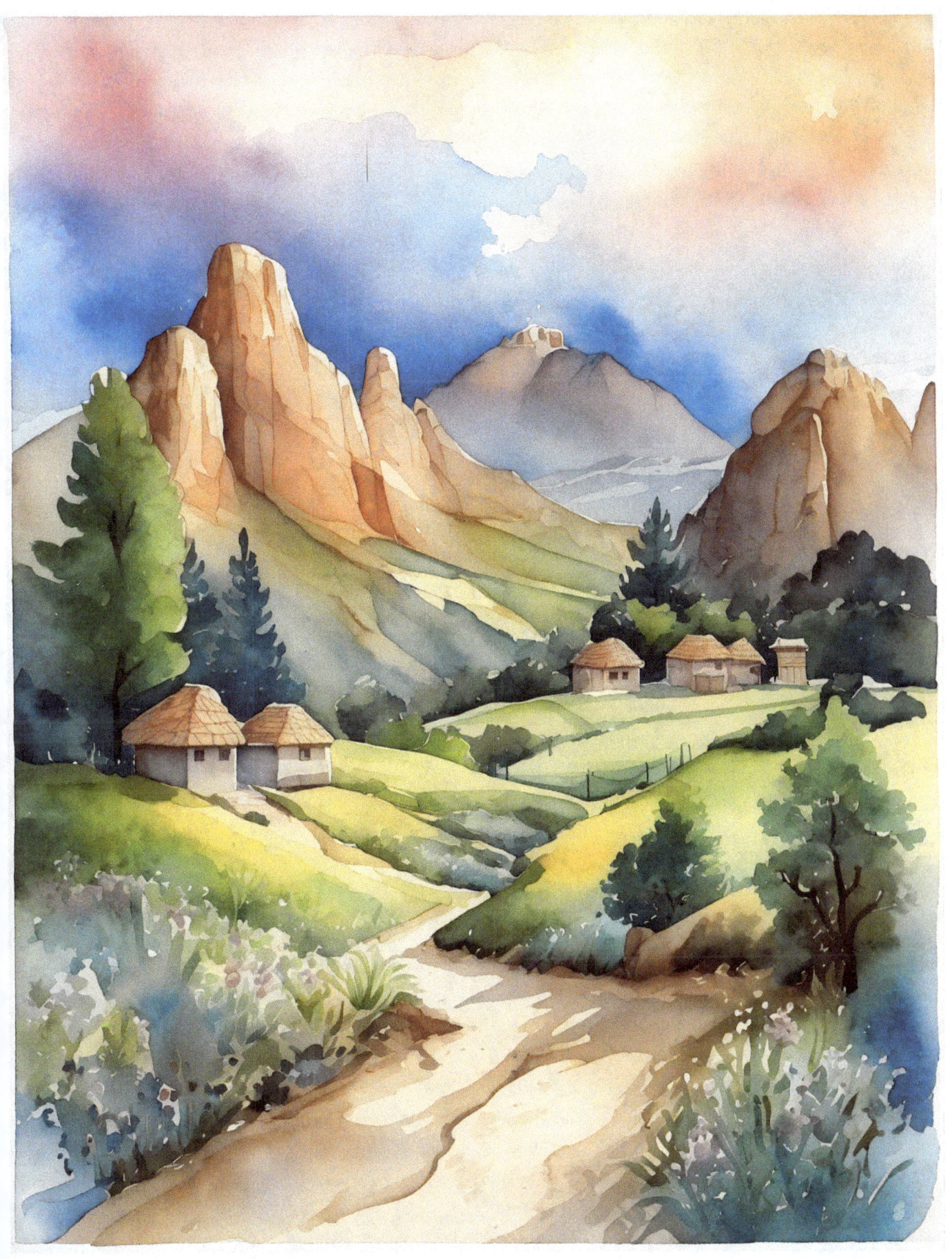

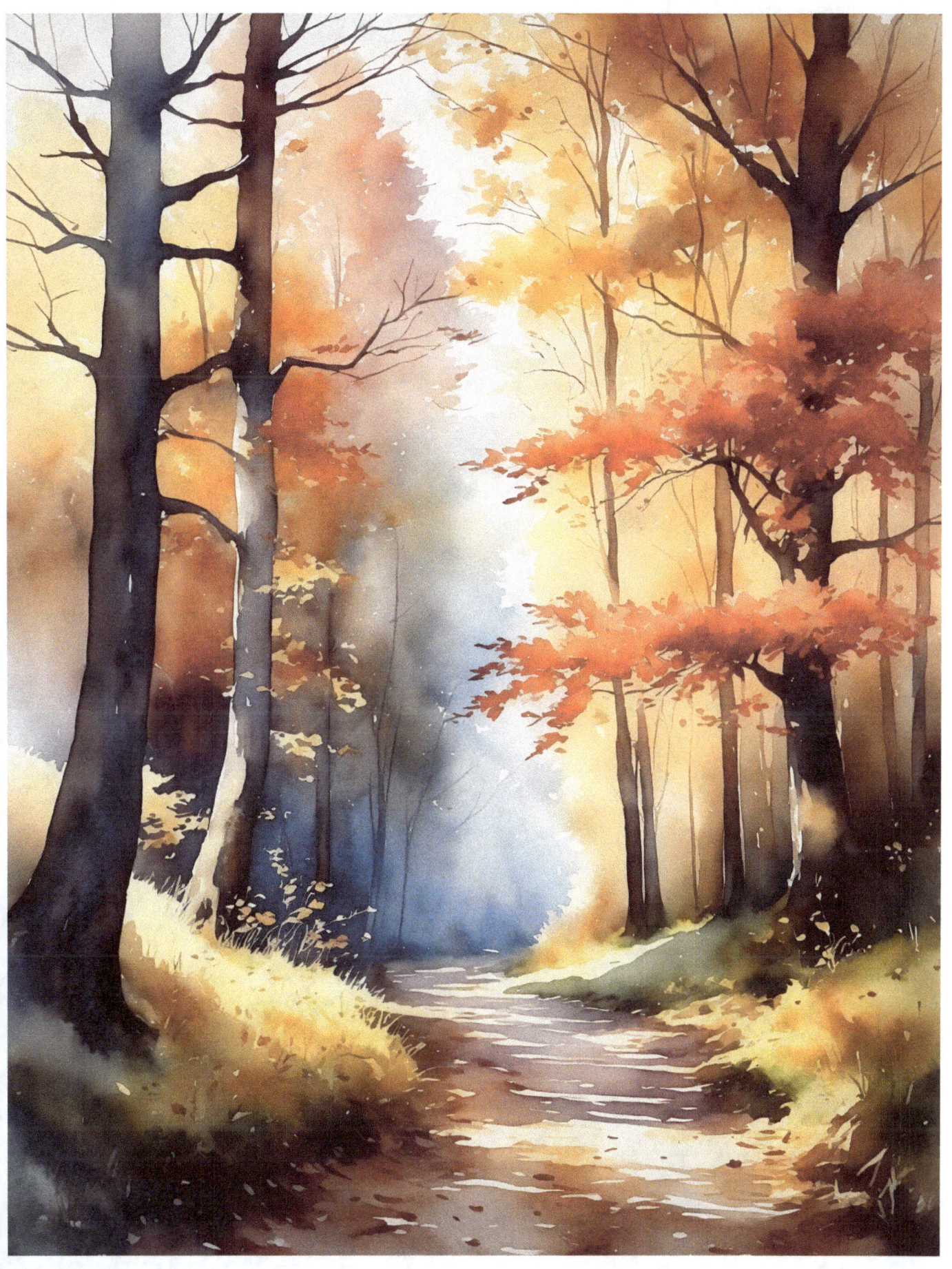

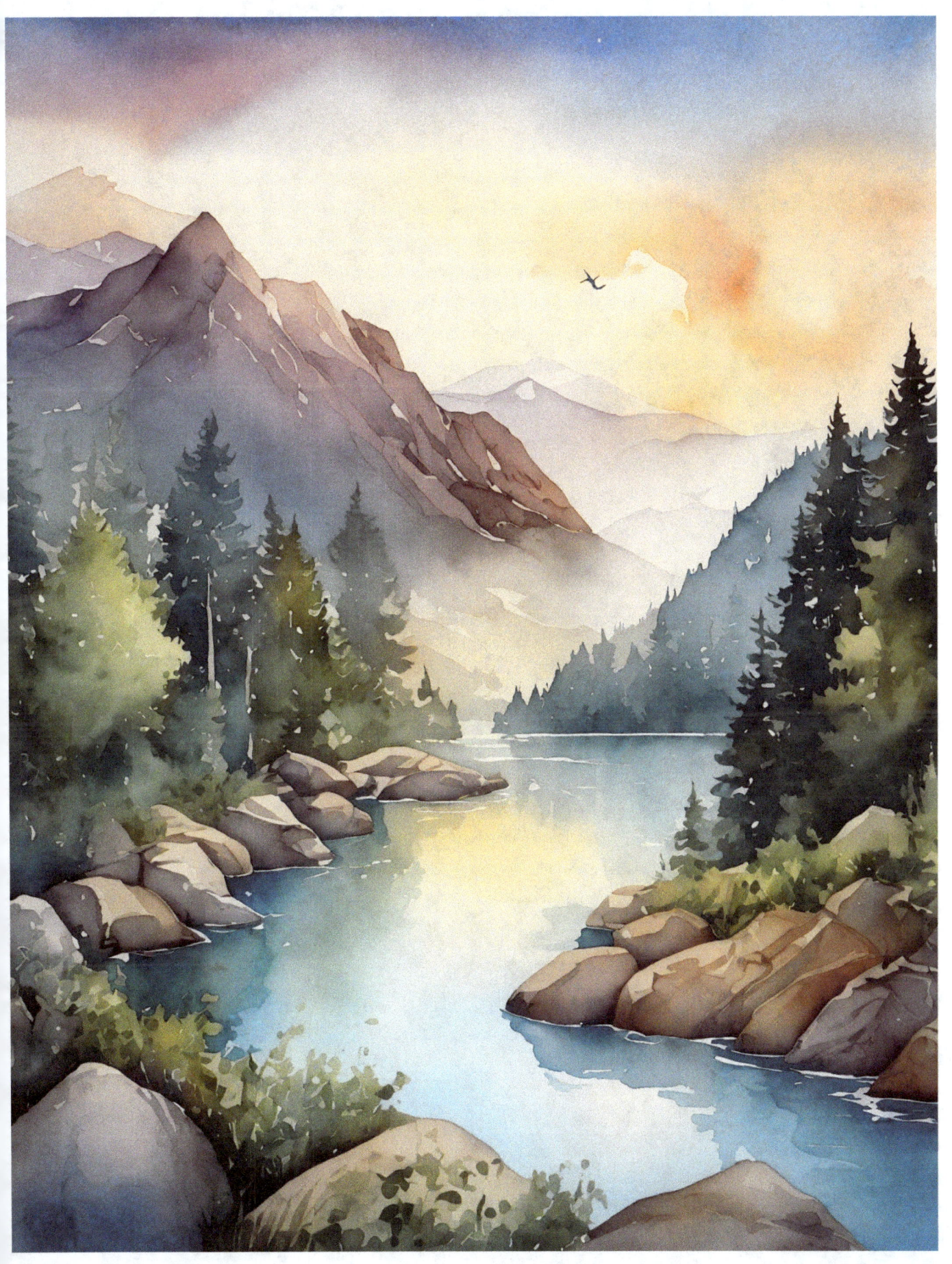

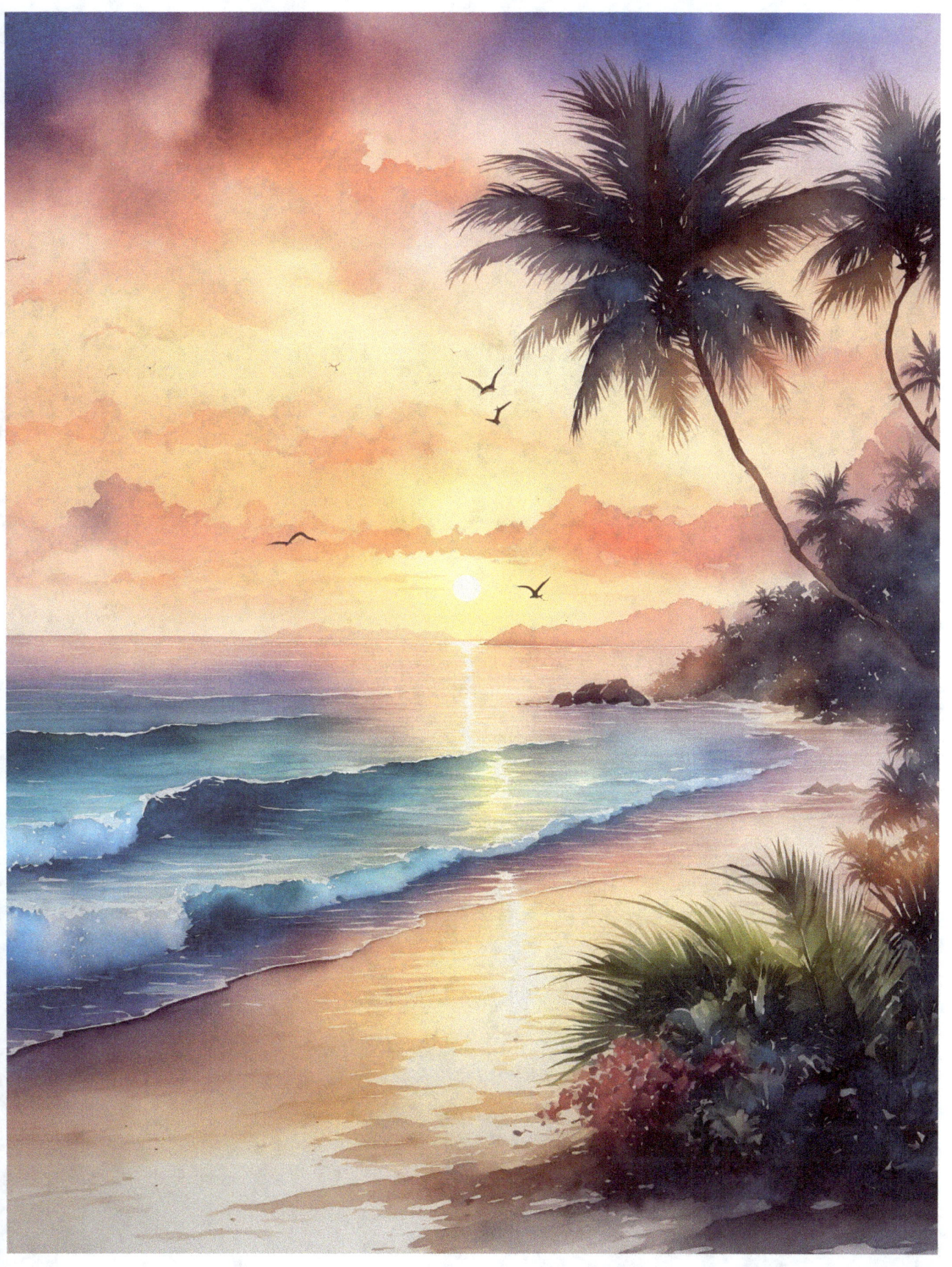

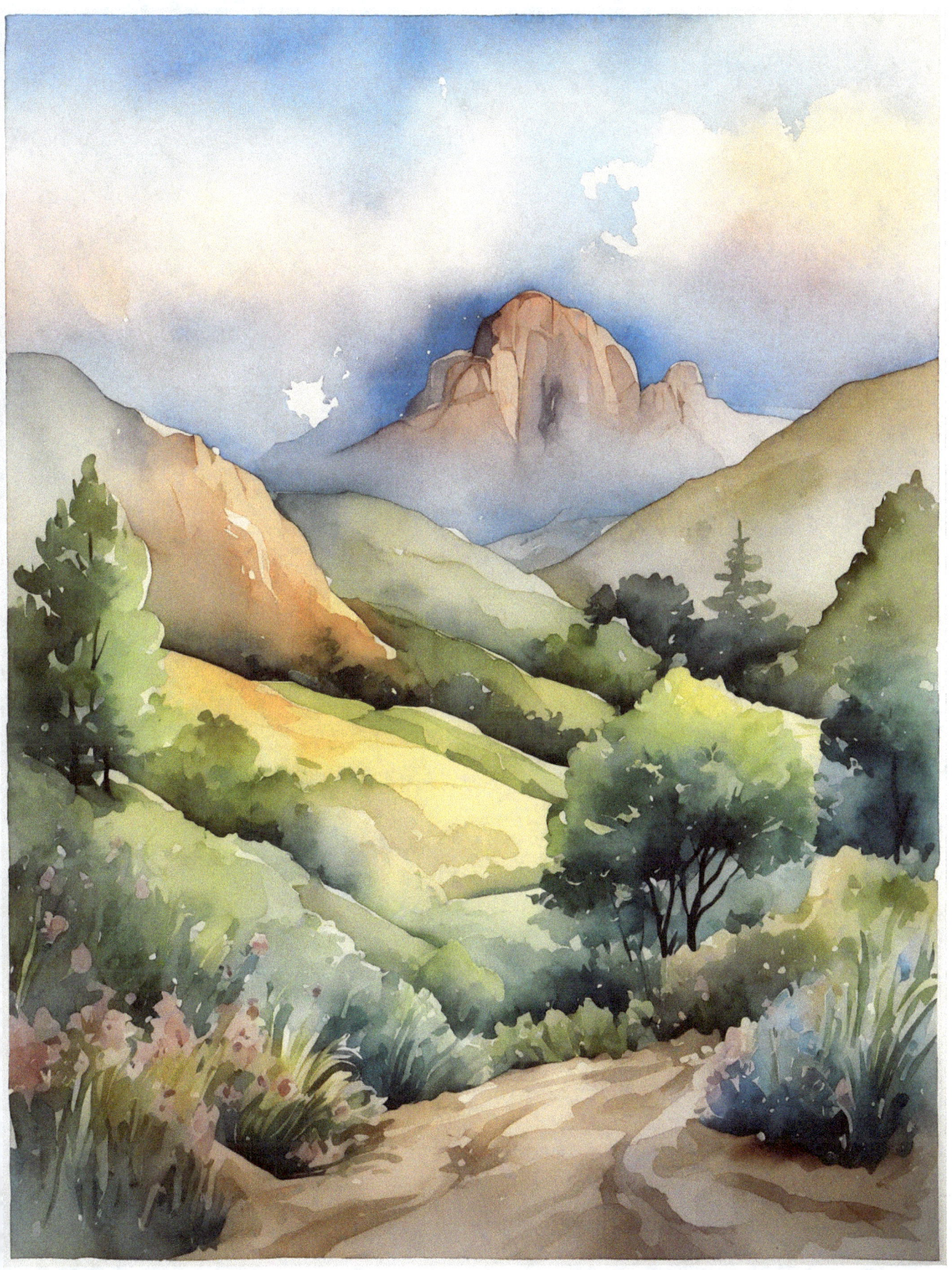

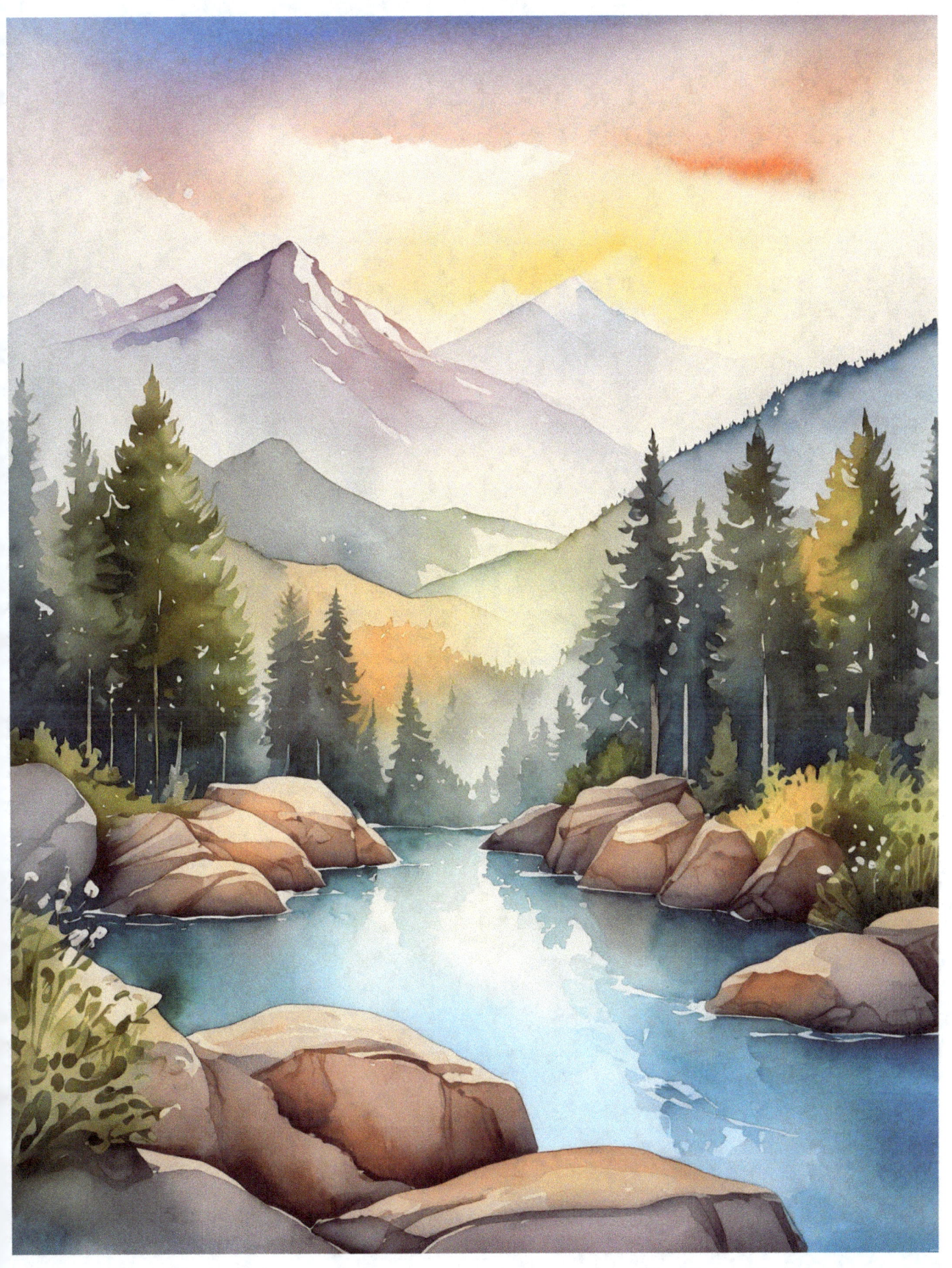

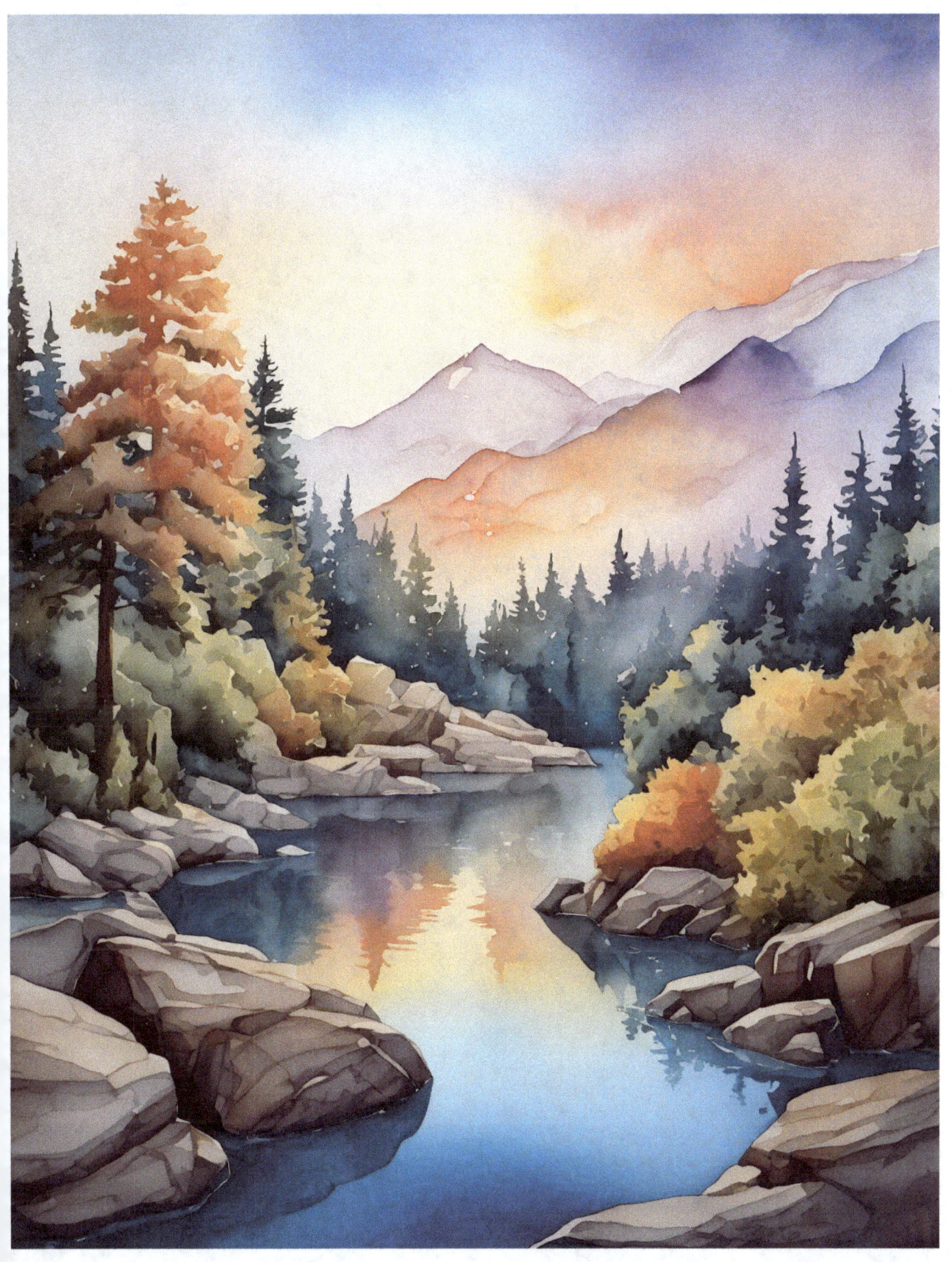

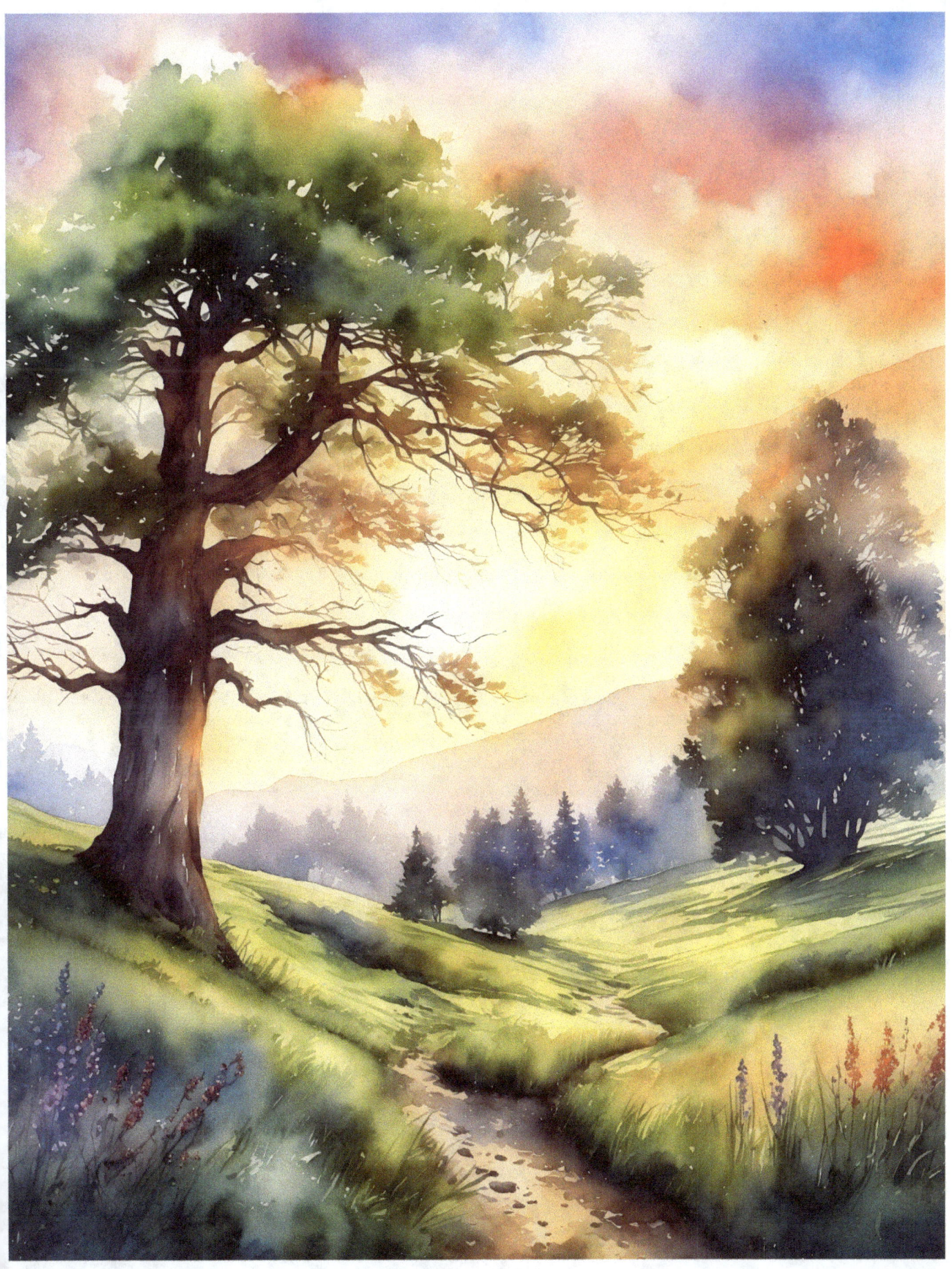

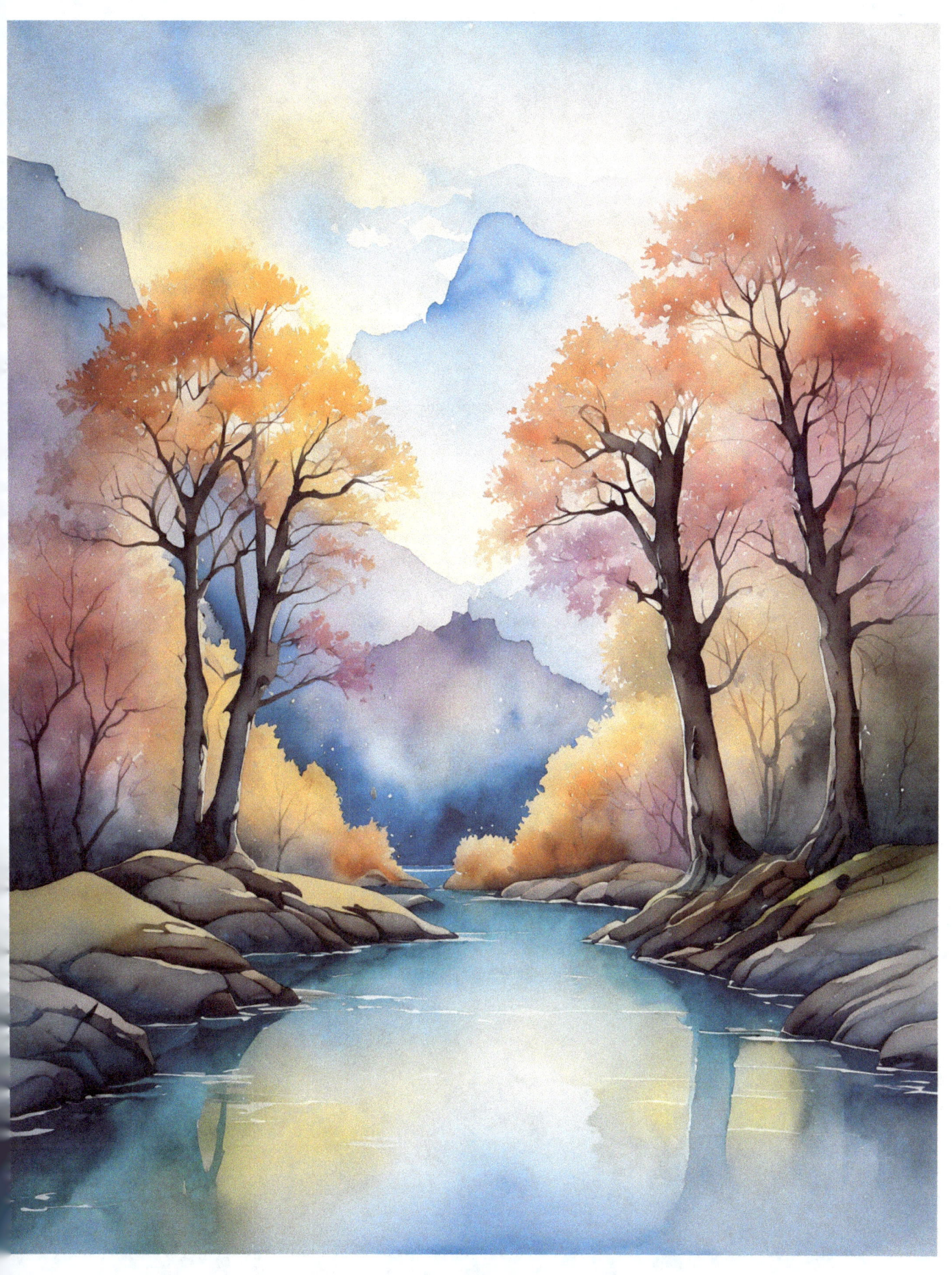

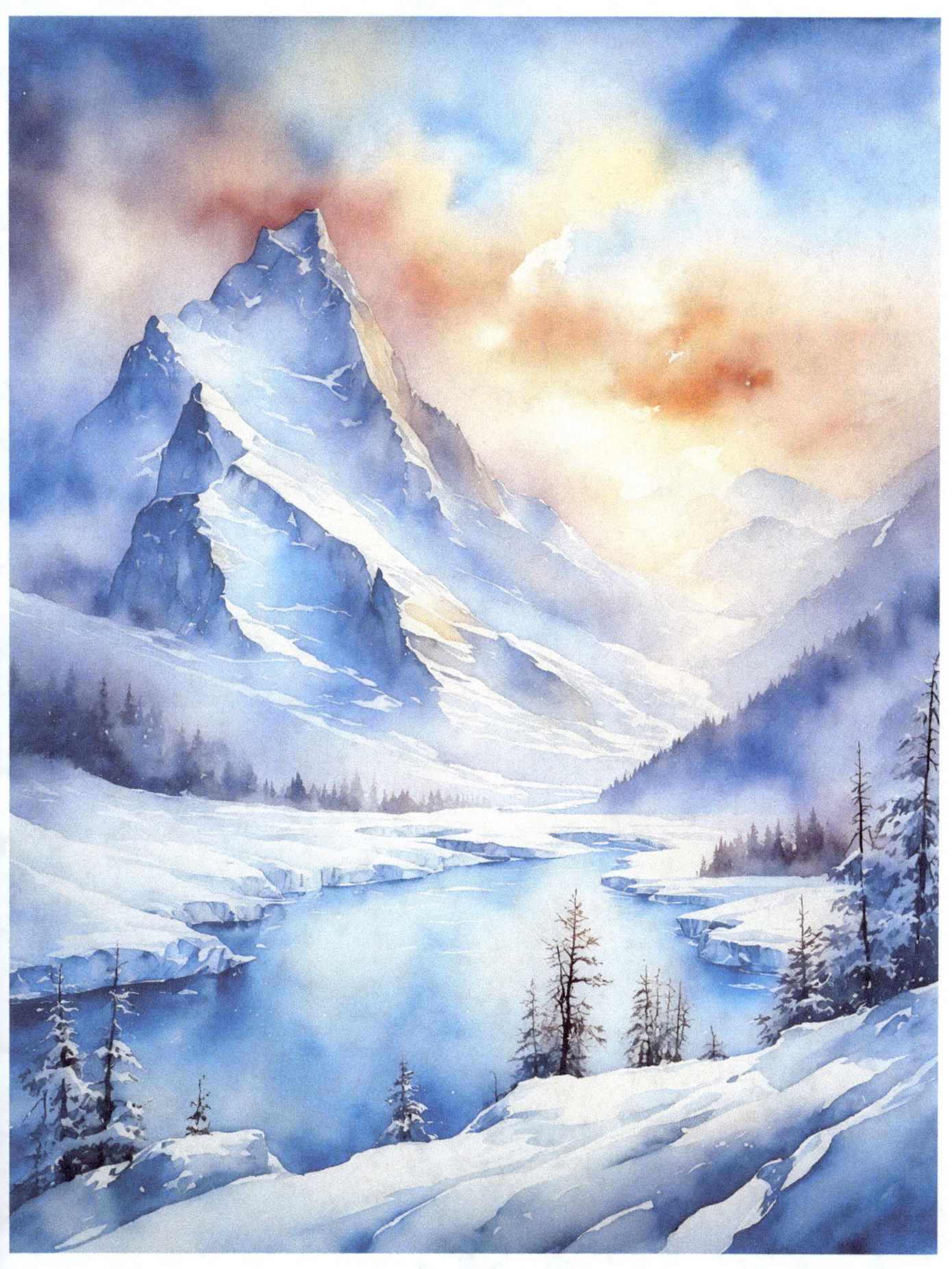

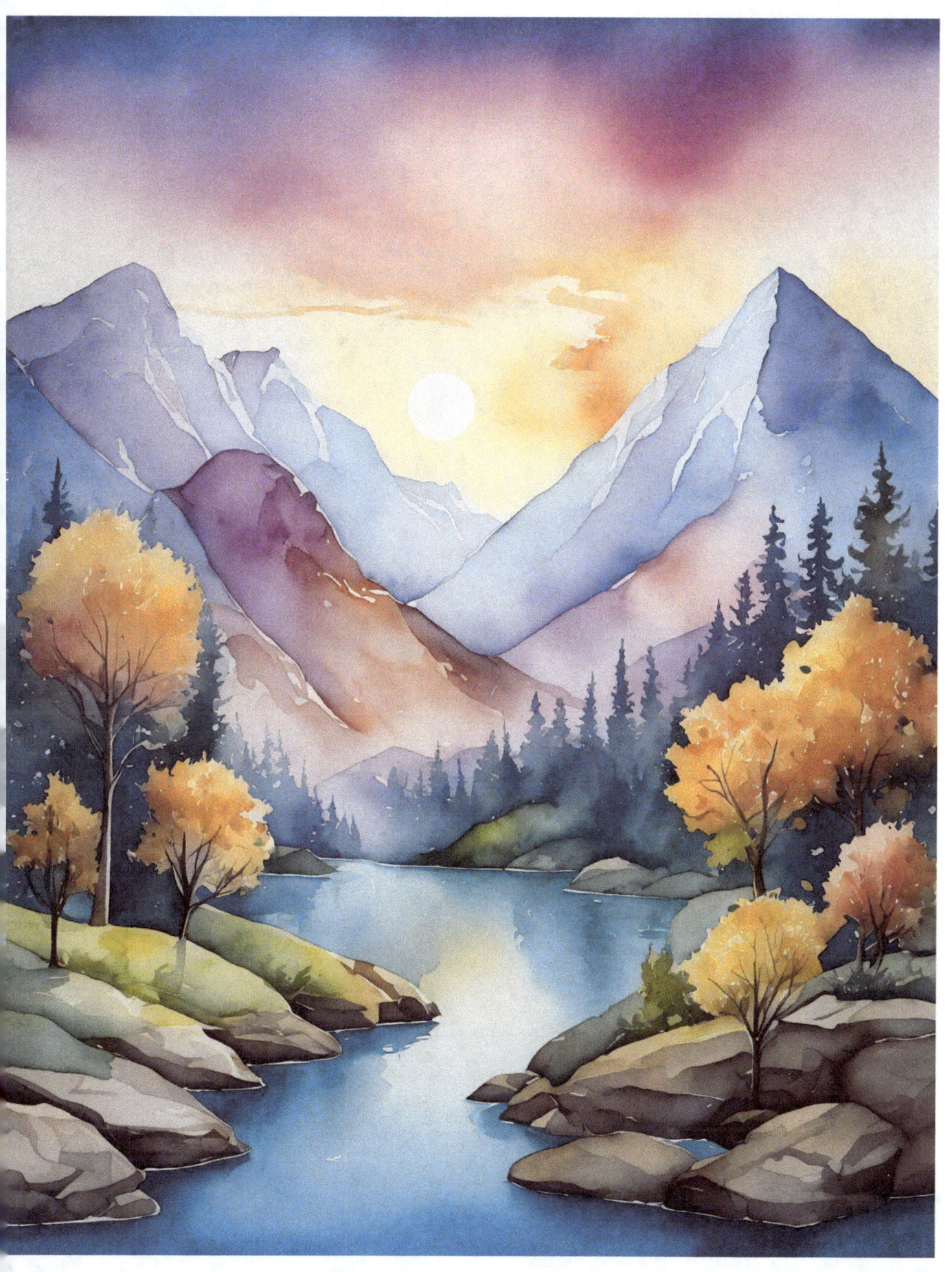

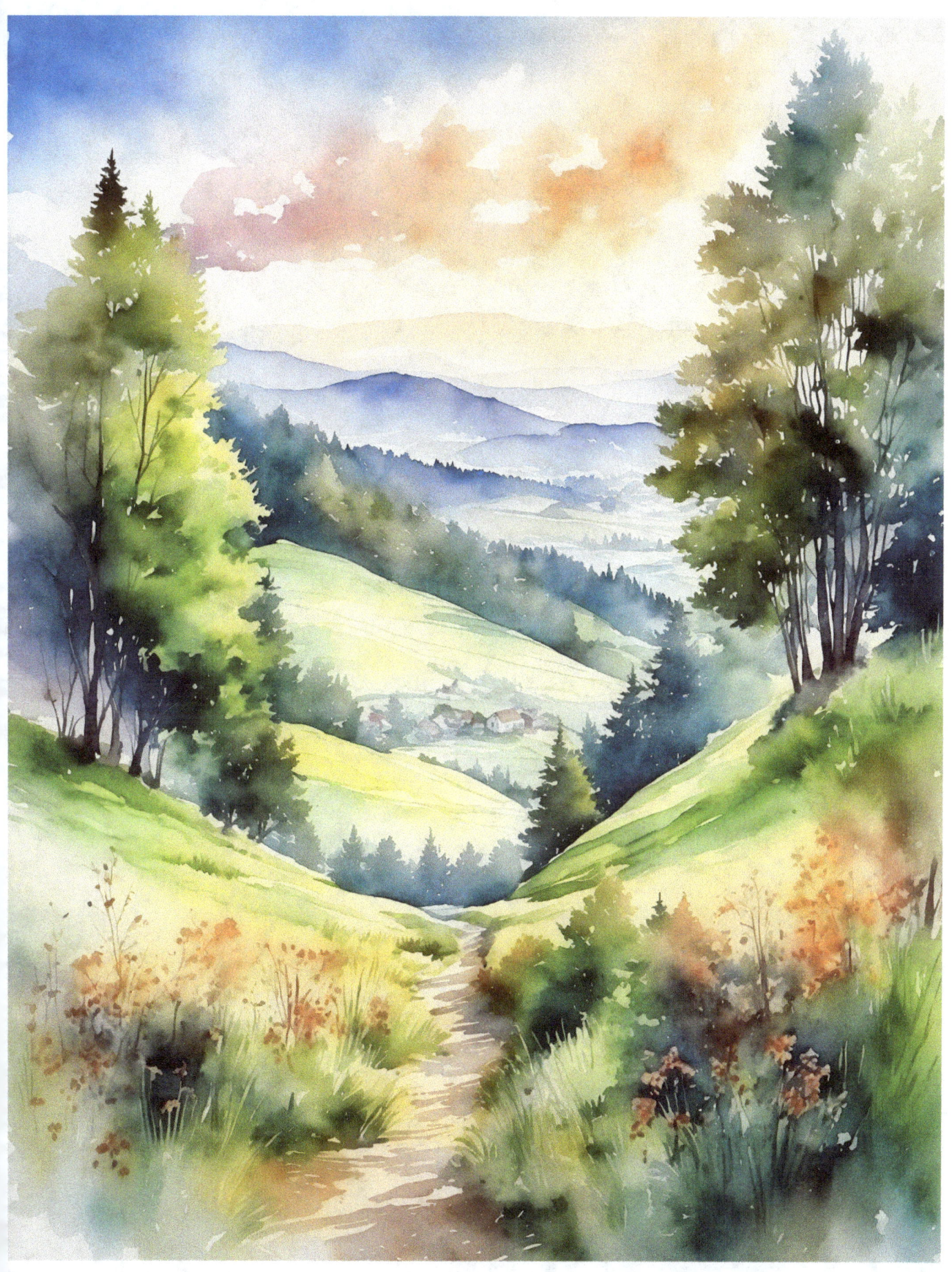

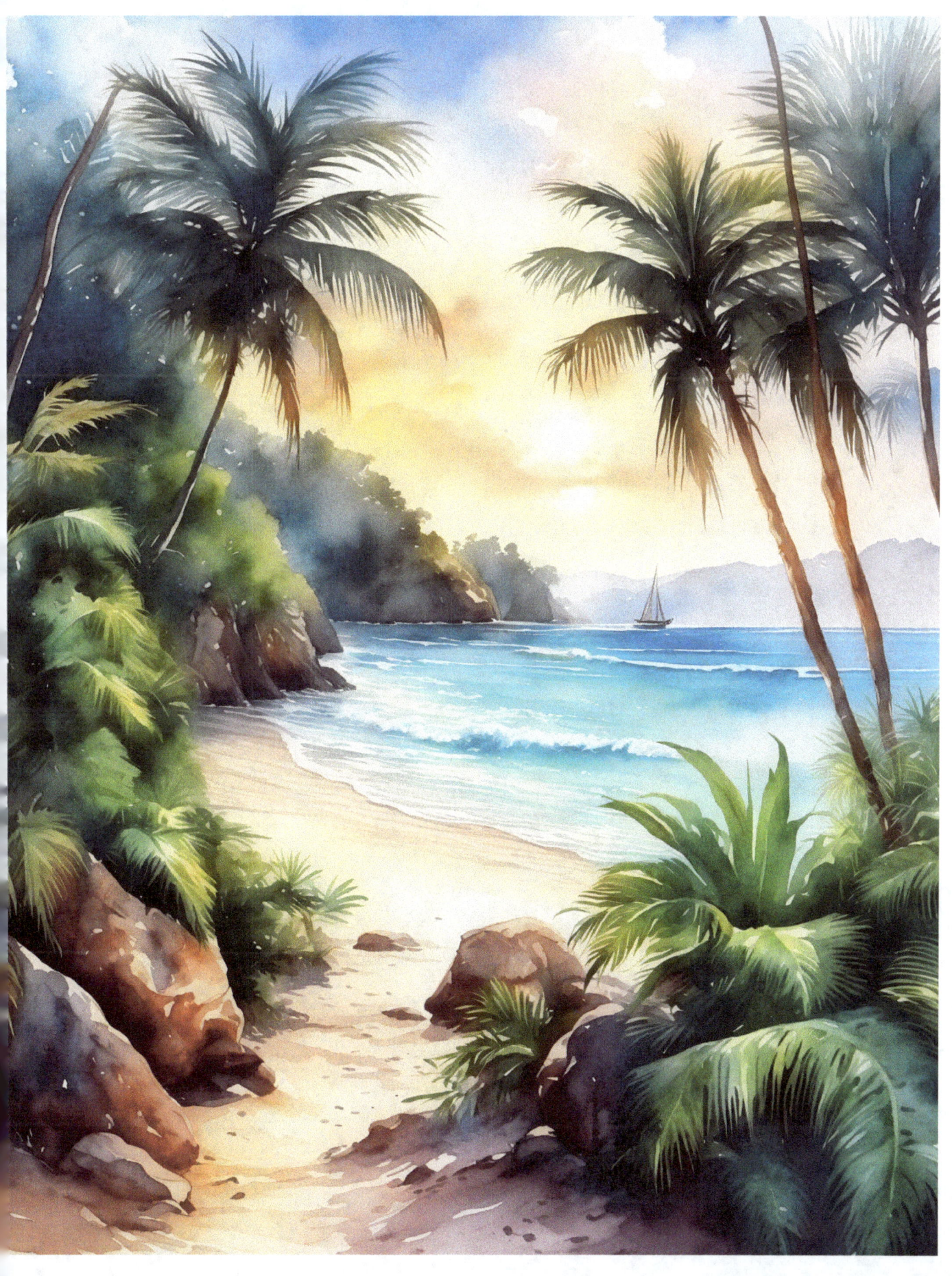

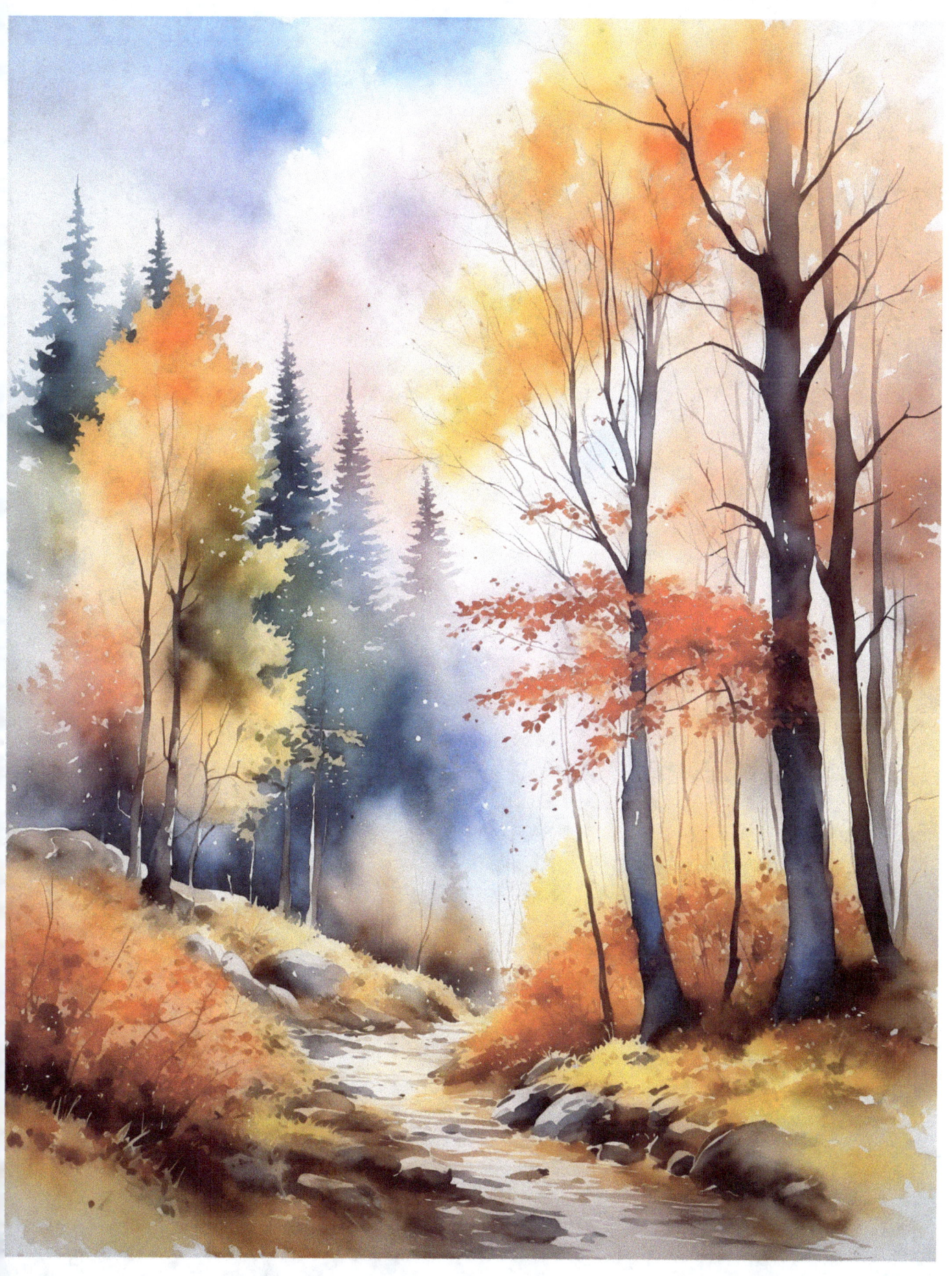

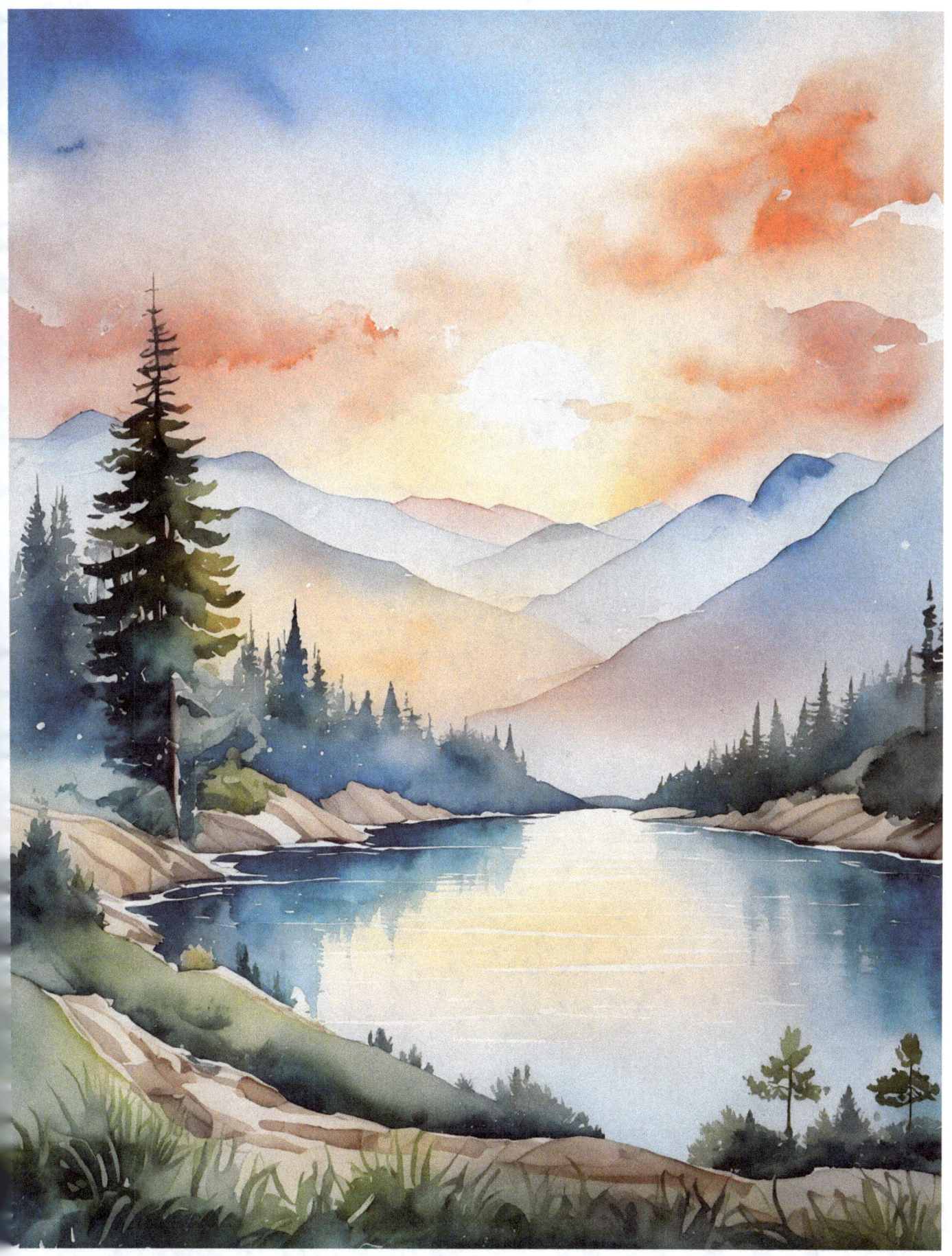

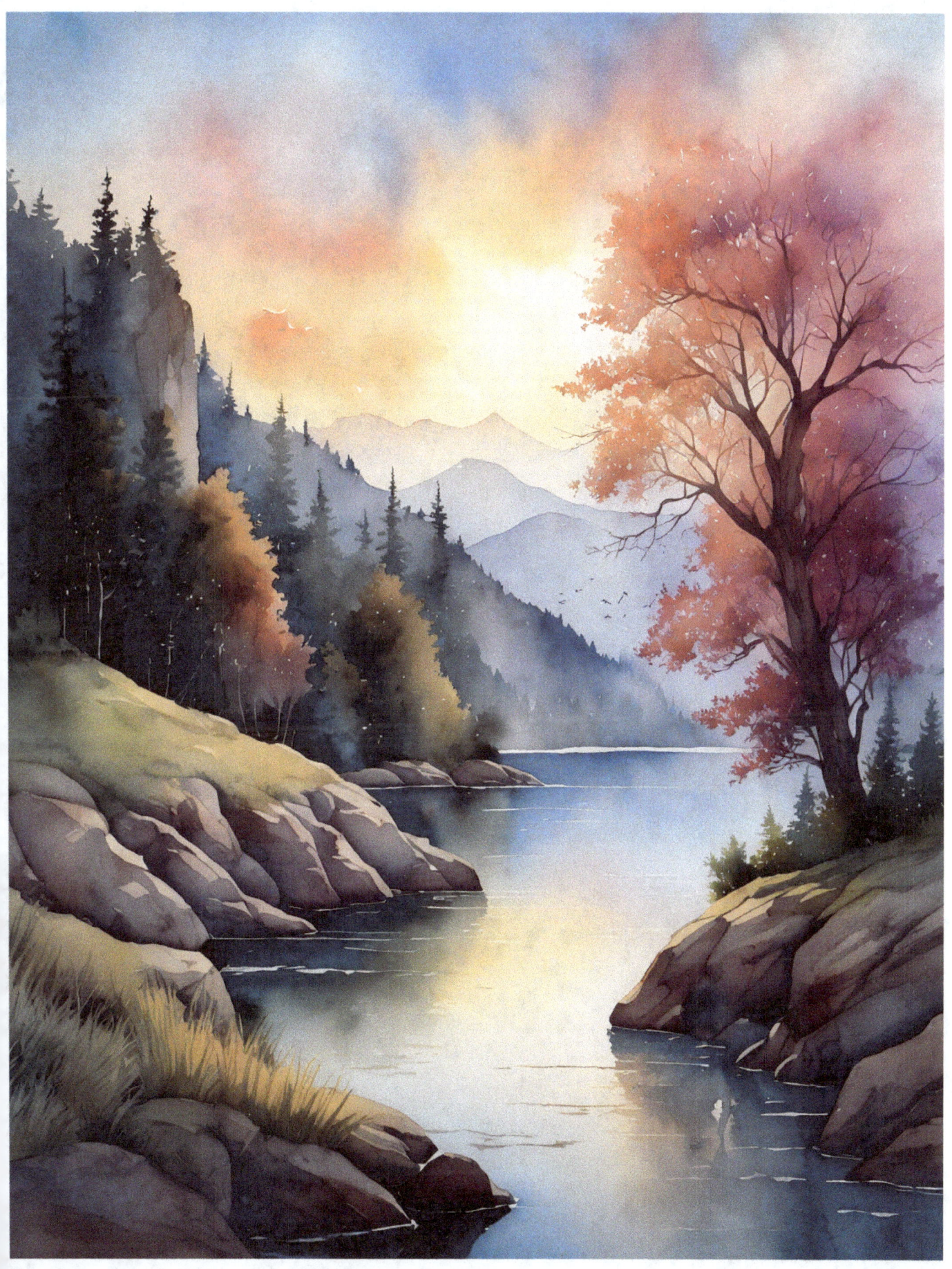

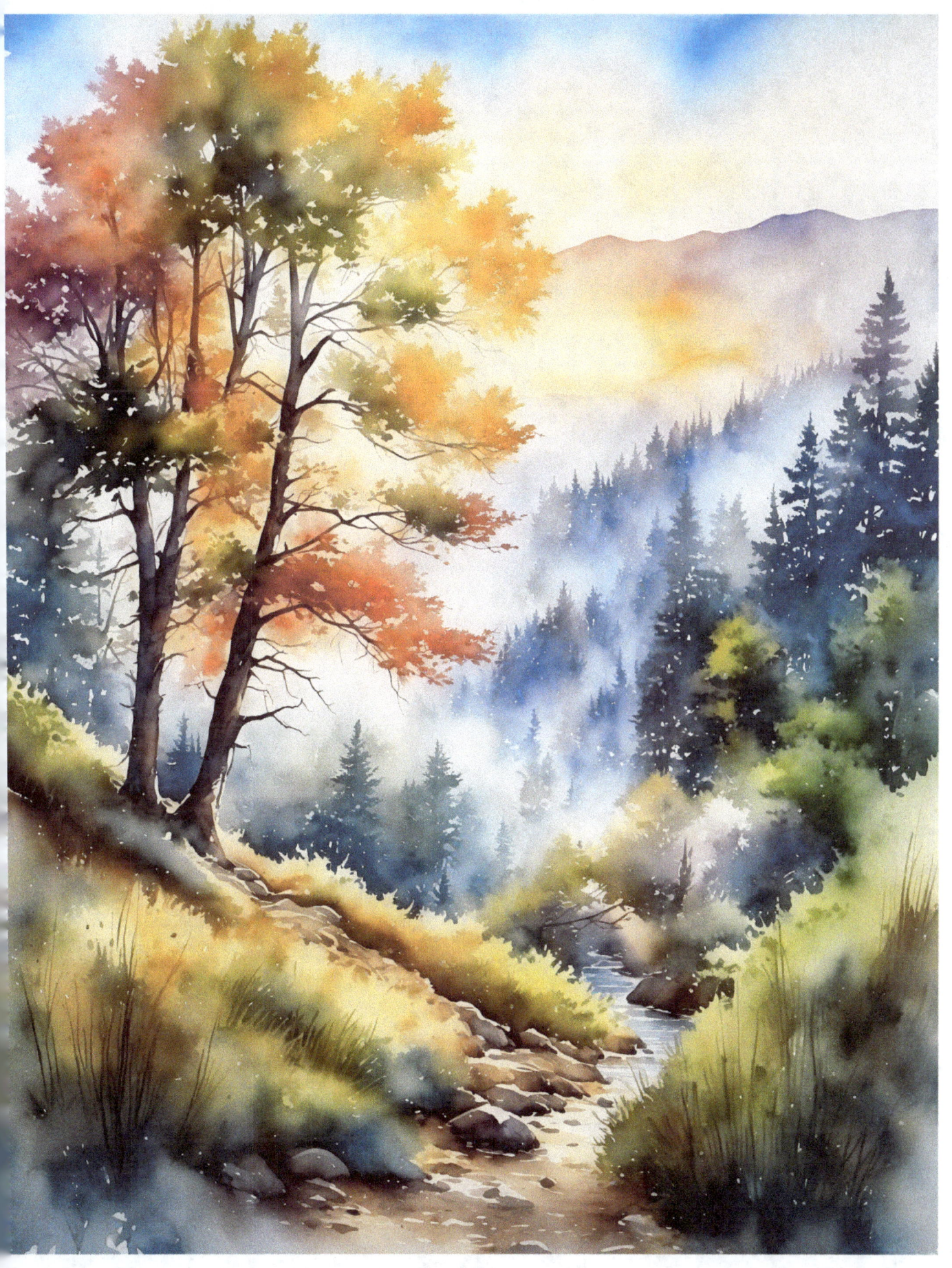

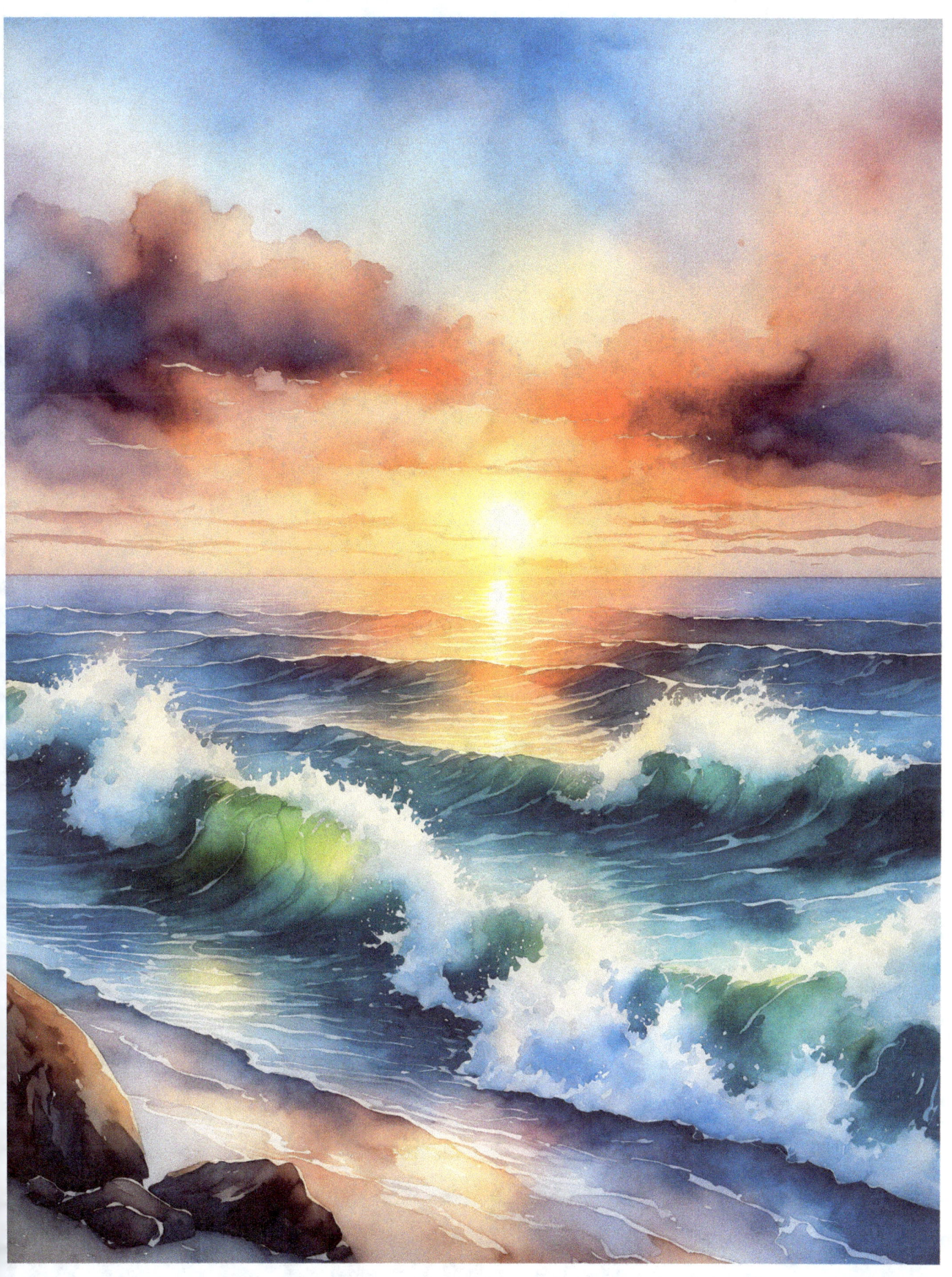

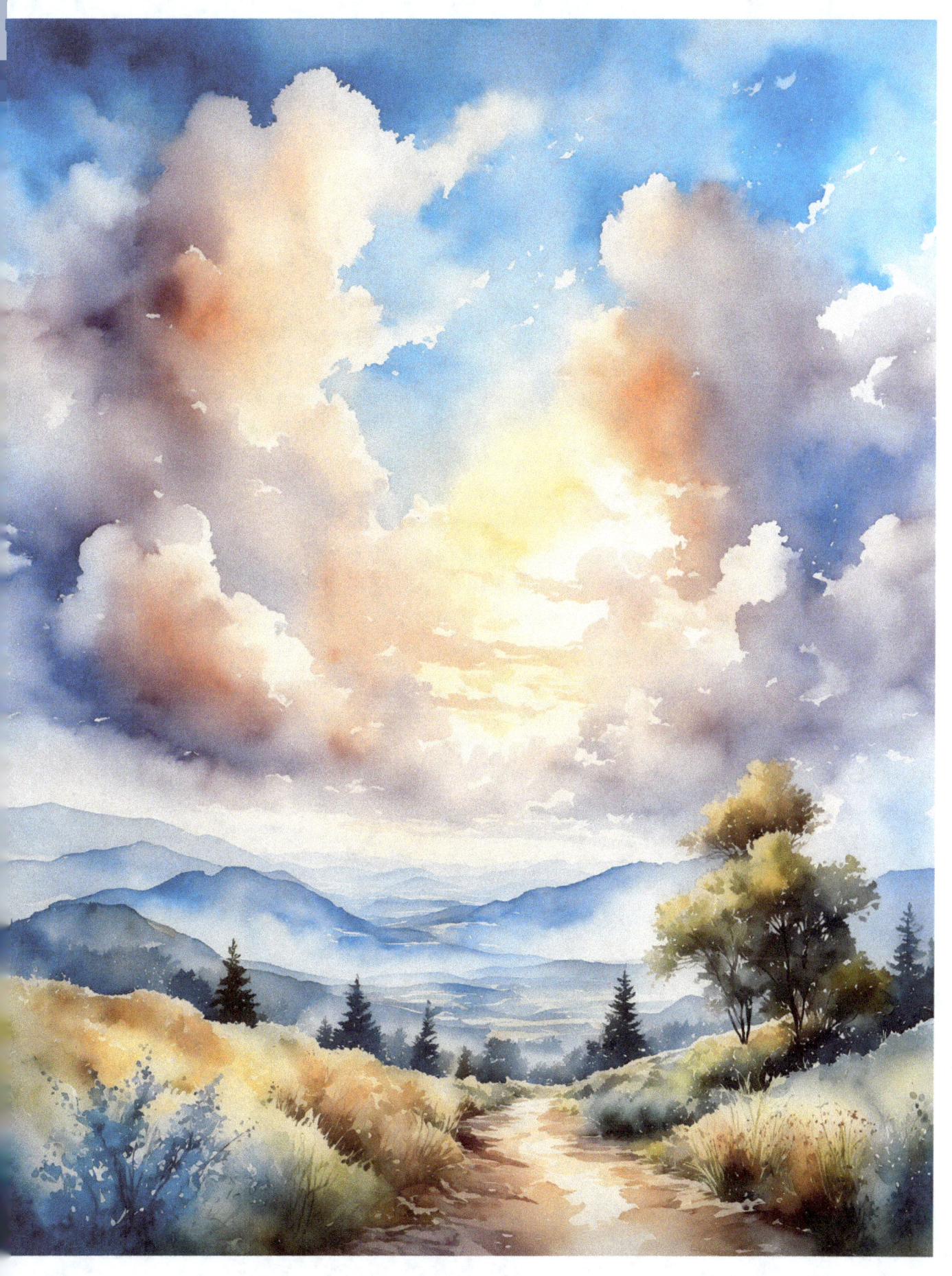

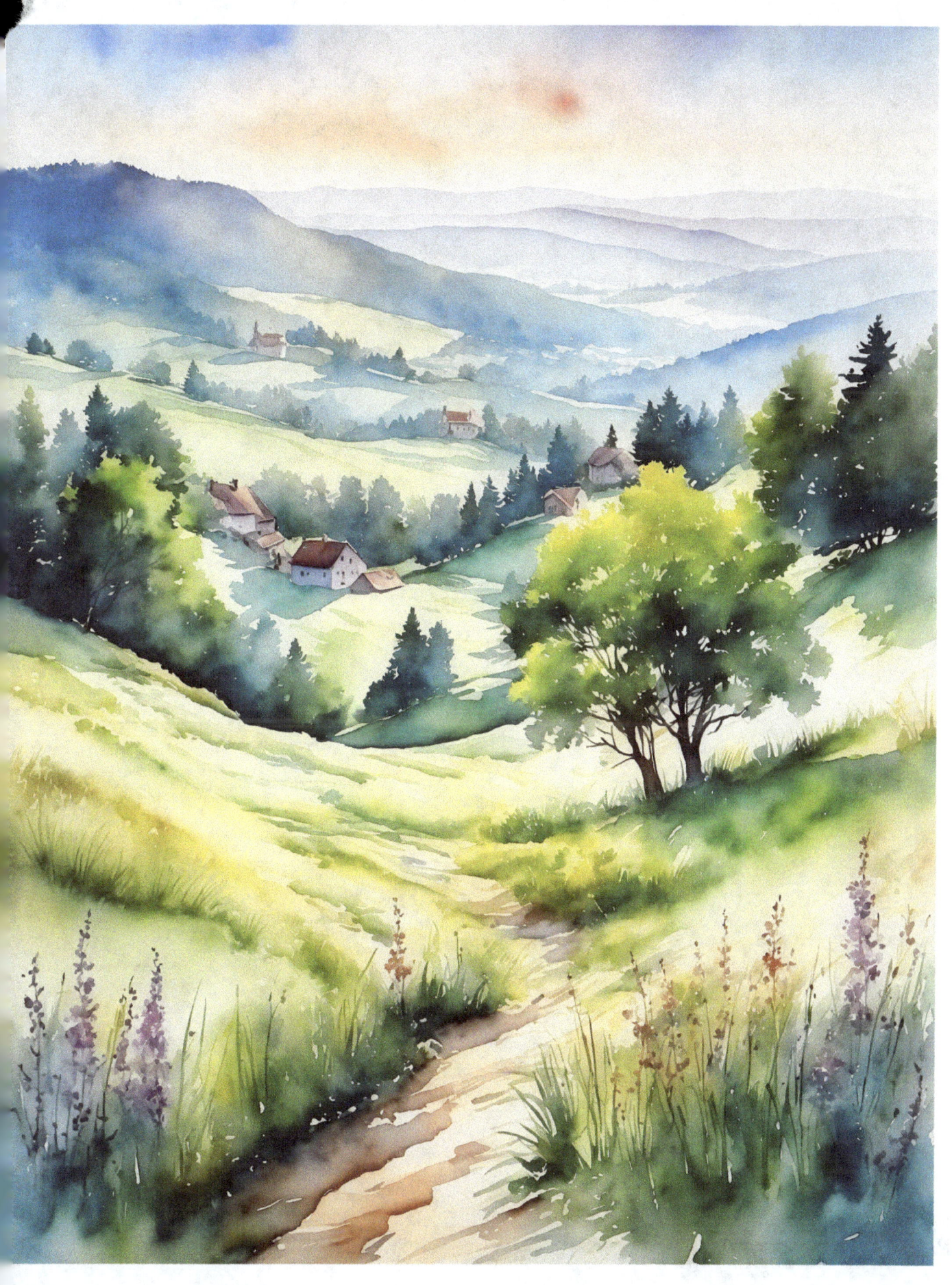

www.ingramcontent.com/pod-product-compliance
Lightning Source LLC
Chambersburg PA
CBHW082356220526
45470CB00008B/2765